THE U.S. NAVAL INSTITUTE ON
THE U.S. NAVY RESERVE

U.S. NAVAL INSTITUTE
Chronicles

For nearly a century and a half since a group of concerned naval officers gathered to provide a forum for the exchange of constructive ideas, the U.S. Naval Institute has been a unique source of information relevant to the nation's sea services. Through the open forum provided by *Proceedings* and *Naval History* magazines, Naval Institute Press (the book-publishing arm of the institute), a robust Oral History program, and more recent immersion in various cyber activities (including the *Naval Institute Blog* and *Naval Institute News*), USNI has built a vast assemblage of intellectual content that has long supported the Navy, Marine Corps, and Coast Guard as well as the nation as a whole.

Recognizing the potential value of this exceptional collection, USNI has embarked on a number of new platforms to reintroduce readers to significant portions of this virtual treasure trove. The U.S. Naval Institute Chronicles series focuses on the relevance of history by resurrecting appropriate selections that are built around various themes, such as battles, personalities, and service components. Available in both paper and eBook versions, these carefully selected volumes help readers navigate through this intellectual labyrinth by providing some of the best contributions that have provided unique perspectives and helped shape naval thinking over the many decades since the institute's founding in 1873.

The U.S. Naval Institute on

THE U.S. NAVY RESERVE

THOMAS J. CUTLER
Series Editor

Naval Institute Press
Annapolis, Maryland

Naval Institute Press
291 Wood Road
Annapolis, MD 21402

Library of Congress Cataloging-in-Publication Data
Names: United States Naval Institute, editor of compilation.
Title: The U.S. Naval Institute on the U.S. Navy Reserve.
Description: Annapolis, Maryland : Naval Institute Press, [2015] | Series:
   U.S. Naval Institute chronicles | Includes bibliographical references.
Identifiers: LCCN 2015040569| ISBN 9781612519906 (hbk. : alk. paper) |
   ISBN 9781612519913 (pdf)
Subjects: LCSH: United States. Naval Reserve.
Classification: LCC VA80 .U45 2015 | DDC 359.3/70973—dc23 LC
   record available at http://lccn.loc.gov/2015040569

♾ Print editions meet the requirements of ANSI/NISO z39.48–1992
(Permanence of Paper).
Printed in the United States of America.

23 22 21 20 19 18 17 16 15   9 8 7 6 5 4 3 2 1
First printing

CONTENTS

Editor's Note xi

Acknowledgments xiii

Introduction 1

1 "A Century of Service" 3
  Vice Admiral Robin Braun, USN
  U.S. Naval Institute *Proceedings*, March 2015

2 "Background for the Future of the U.S. Naval Reserve" 12
  James Hessman
  U.S. Naval Institute *Proceedings*, May 1978

3 "'Let's Get the Yale Gang'" 17
  Rear Admiral Joseph F. Callo, USNR (Ret.)
  U.S. Naval Institute *Proceedings*, September 2001

4 "The Naval Reserve Officers' Training Corps" 25
  Captain C. W. Nimitz, USN
  U.S. Naval Institute *Proceedings*, June 1928

5 "Notes on U.S. Naval Reserve Aviation" 36
  Lieutenant Commander J. B. Lynch, A-O, USNR
  U.S. Naval Institute *Proceedings*, April 1939

6 "The Corn Belt Navy" 47
    Lieutenant Ralph C. Lowes Jr., DE-O, USNR
    U.S. Naval Institute *Proceedings*, April 1939

7 "'A Project So Unique'" 58
    A. Denis Clift
    U.S. Naval Institute *Proceedings*, June 2014

8 "World War II Subchasers" 67
    Theodore R. Treadwell
    Selections from chapters 2, 3, and 4 of *Splinter Fleet:*
    The Wooden Subchasers of World War II,
    Naval Institute Press, 2000

9 "Future of the Naval Reserve" 92
    Captain Paul P. Blackburn, USN (Ret.)
    U.S. Naval Institute *Proceedings*, March 1945

10 "Standby Squadron" 108
    Lieutenant W. H. Vernor Jr., USNR
    U.S. Naval Institute *Proceedings*, July 1952

11 "The Naval Reserve Should Work" 125
    Captain James G. Abert, USNR
    U.S. Naval Institute *Proceedings*, February 1980

12 "The Reserve's Biggest Problem" 136
    Vice Admiral Robert F. Dunn, USN
    U.S. Naval Institute *Proceedings*, October 1984

13 "Why Not One Navy" 147
    Captain Harlan B. Miller, USNR (Ret.)
    U.S. Naval Institute *Proceedings*, October 1990

14 "The Selected Reserve: The Peace Dividend" 156
    Robert D. Helsel
    U.S. Naval Institute *Proceedings*, October 1990

15 "The NRF Has More to Offer" 160
    Lieutenant Commander William D. Schubert Jr., USNR
    U.S. Naval Institute *Proceedings*, October 1990

16 "Navy's Reserve Will Be Integrated with Active Forces" 164
    Rear Admiral David O. Anderson, USN, and
    Rear Admiral J. A. Winnefeld, USN
    U.S. Naval Institute *Proceedings*, November 2004

    Index 169

EDITOR'S NOTE

BECAUSE THIS BOOK is an anthology, containing documents from different time periods, the selections included here are subject to varying styles and conventions. Other variables are introduced by the evolving nature of the Naval Institute's publication practices. For those reasons, certain editorial decisions were required in order to avoid introducing confusion or inconsistencies and to expedite the process of assembling these sometimes disparate pieces.

Gender

Most jarring of the differences that readers will encounter are likely those associated with gender. A number of the included selections were written when the armed forces were primarily a male domain and so adhere to purely masculine references. I have chosen to leave the original language intact in these documents for the sake of authenticity and to avoid the complications that can arise when trying to make anachronistic adjustments. So readers are asked to "translate" (converting the ubiquitous "he" to "he or she" and "his" to "her or his" as required) and, while doing so, to celebrate the progress that we have made in these matters in more recent times.

Author "Biographies"

Another problem arises when considering biographical information of the various authors whose works make up this special collection. Some of the selections included in this anthology were originally accompanied by biographical information about their authors. Others were not. Those "biographies" that do exist have been included. They pertain to the time the article was written and may vary in terms of length and depth, some amounting to a single sentence pertaining to the author's current duty station, others consisting of several paragraphs that cover the author's career.

Ranks

I have retained the ranks of the authors *at the time of their publication.* As noted above, some of the authors wrote early in their careers, and the sagacity of their earlier contributions says much about the individuals, about the significance of the Naval Institute's forum, and about the importance of writing to the naval services—something that is sometimes underappreciated.

Other Anomalies

Readers may detect some inconsistencies in editorial style, reflecting staff changes at the Naval Institute, evolving practices in publishing itself, and various other factors not always identifiable. Some of the selections will include citational support, others will not. Authors sometimes coined their own words and occasionally violated traditional style conventions. *Bottom line:* with the exception of the removal of some extraneous materials (such as section numbers from book excerpts) and the conversion to a consistent font and overall design, these articles and excerpts appear as they originally did when first published.

ACKNOWLEDGMENTS

THIS PROJECT would not be possible without the dedication and remarkable industry of Denis Clift, the Naval Institute's vice president for planning and operations and president emeritus of the National Intelligence University. This former naval officer, who served in the administrations of eleven successive U.S. presidents and was once editor in chief of *Proceedings* magazine, bridged the gap between paper and electronics by single-handedly reviewing the massive body of the Naval Institute's intellectual content to find many of the treasures included in this anthology.

A great deal is also owed to Mary Ripley, Janis Jorgensen, Rebecca Smith, Judy Heise, Debbie Smith, Elaine Davy, and Heather Lancaster who devoted many hours and much talent to the digitization project that is at the heart of these anthologies.

Introduction

IT HAS BEEN 100 years since the founding of the U.S. Navy Reserve (then-called the *Naval* Reserve). In that time, Navy Reserve Sailors have served in every conflict from World War I to the present and have provided continuity and peace of mind in the interim years of peace. A little-known but important fact is that the vast majority of Sailors who served in World War II and ultimately achieved the greatest victory at sea in history were reserves serving on active duty.

From its earliest days, the Navy Reserve has often been a central subject in *Proceedings* magazine, and the exploits of Navy Reserve Sailors have many times been chronicled in the pages of Naval Institute Press books and *Naval History* magazine articles. From that vast library have been culled the articles and excerpts presented in this edition of *Naval Institute Chronicles*. Whether these selections are read cover-to-cover or selectively, readers will find much information along with substantial doses of inspiration as the importance of this vital component of the Navy is revealed and celebrated.

1

"A Century of Service"

Vice Admiral Robin Braun, USN

U.S. Naval Institute *Proceedings*
(March 2015): 18–22

AS THE NAVY RESERVE recognizes its centennial on 3 March, we celebrate 100 years of dedicated service to the Navy and the nation. In every conflict from World War I to the present, Navy Reserve sailors have answered the call to serve. Since its inception, the organization's size, structure, and operational employment have continuously evolved as directed by political and Navy leadership in response to Fleet requirements. Yet today's Navy Reserve is arguably the most operationally experienced and integrated force in its history, with thousands of sailors having mobilized to support Fleet and combatant commander requirements over the past 13 years.

A Proud History

Some may be surprised that the Navy Reserve is only a century old, while the Navy recently celebrated its 239th birthday. That's because from the American Revolution through the Civil War, the Navy employed merchant sailors and civilian volunteers to provide additional manpower during wartime. This arrangement worked well until the Fleet began transitioning from wood to steel warships at the end of the 19th century, when the need for a specially trained and reliable reserve force became apparent. Several attempts to create a federal naval reserve failed, leaving the solution to the states. Massachusetts established the first naval militia, and by 1914 more than 7,500 sailors were serving in 22 state naval militias. These received federal funding and obsolete naval vessels for training but remained under state control. State naval militias were mobilized and placed under federal control during the Spanish-American War.

As successful as these units were in that confict, the outbreak of World War I in 1914 demonstrated that prosecuting a modern war at sea required a professional federal naval reserve force. A campaign in Congress to appropriate funding for such a force brought passage of legislation on 3 March 1915 to establish the U.S. Naval Reserve. At first only recently honorably discharged enlisted sailors could enroll, which severely limited the pool of recruits. Reorganized in 1916 as the U.S. Naval Reserve Force, new policies allowed for the enrollment of citizens without prior service—including women—and the commissioning of officers below the rank of lieutenant commander. When the United States entered World War I in April 1917, 8,000 sailors were members of the Naval Reserve Force; 18 months later, more than 250,000 Reserve sailors were on active duty—including 11,000 women—making up more than half the wartime Navy.

Naval Reserve sailors on board the USS *Ward* (DD-139) fired the first shots of the war in the Pacific in the early-morning hours of 7 December 1941. The *Ward* was on patrol outside Pearl Harbor when she engaged and sank a Japanese mini submarine two hours before the main Japanese air attack began. With these opening salvos, the Reserve sailors on board the *Ward* became the first Navy personnel to see action in World War II. Over the next few weeks, thousands of men and women joined the Naval Reserve. Its sailors participated in every major campaign of the war. They served on surface ships and submarines, and as aviators and Seabees. Officer and enlisted women accepted for volunteer emergency service filled critical roles at shore installations, releasing men for duty at sea. Naval Reserve nurses cared for sailors and Marines at home and on the battlefield. Five future U.S. presidents served as Reserve officers during World War II and 15 Reserve sailors received the Medal of Honor for heroic actions. When the United States entered World War II, 45,000 Reserve sailors were serving on active duty. Four years later, more than 3 million reservists were serving, comprising 84 percent of the total force.

The Korean War's eruption in June 1950 required the mobilization of more than 170,000 Naval Reserve sailors over the next three years. Many served on front-line warships and in tactical aviation squadrons operating off the coast of Korea. Reserve hospital corpsmen performed arduous duties in austere field hospitals and while embedded with Marine Corps infantry units. In the decades following the Korean War, Naval Reserve forces were mobilized as needed to help counter the spread of communism. In 1961 the Berlin Crisis triggered the activation of 40 Naval Reserve Force ships and three reserve squadrons. Six years later, two Reserve Seabee battalions deployed to South Vietnam. During that time, Naval Reserve transport squadrons flew thousands of air-logistics missions to and from the Vietnam theater.

The Naval Reserve's mission transformed in the post-Vietnam era from generally functioning as a strategic augmentation force that mirrored the active component's structure into a more specialized, capabilities-based force. Sailors still served on Naval Reserve Force ships and in Reserve naval aviation squadrons, but new missions evolved or expanded, including cargo handling, intelligence, naval-coastal warfare, and mobile construction.

Budget cuts in 1977 reduced Reserve end strength from 129,000 to 87,000. Then in the 1980s, as President Ronald Reagan pursued a 600-ship Navy to counter the Soviet Union, the Naval Reserve under Secretary John Lehman, a reserve naval aviator himself, expanded to almost 150,000 to help support the Fleet.

Operations Desert Shield and Desert Storm resulted in the largest mobilization of the Naval Reserve since the Korean War. Over 20,000 Reserve sailors deployed to Southwest Asia to provide surge support and expertise in port security, field medicine, air logistics, and mobile construction. In the following years, the Reserve settled into a battle rhythm common for a strategic force after a significant mobilization. Reserve sailors focused on maintaining operational and strategic readiness, using their annual complement of inactive duty-training periods and annual training days. Smaller-scale voluntary mobilizations and recalls supported contingencies and crisis-response operations in areas including the Balkans and Haiti.

9/11: A New Era of Service

The events of 9/11 sparked another large-scale reserve mobilization that continues today. In the aftermath of the attacks, President George W. Bush approved an order to call up to 50,000 Reservists from all service components to active duty. Within months, over 9,000 Reserve sailors were supporting homeland defense and Navy and combatant commands worldwide. Immediately after the attacks, Navy Reservists were posted at bases across the country to stand security watches. Within days, operational planners surged forward to bolster the 5th Fleet and Central Command staffs. Reserve naval coastal warfare units were mobilized to provide port security and eventually guard captured Iraqi ports and oil terminals.

Among the first troops to arrive in Afghanistan at Camp Rhino and the Kandahar airport in late 2001 were active and reserve Seabees, some of whom deployed within 24 hours of notification. They helped Brigadier General James Mattis' Marines of Task Force 58 to press their amphibious assault 350 miles inland from the Arabian Sea. During the early days of Operation Enduring Freedom, the Seabees worked 24 hours a day to keep Camp Rhino and the Kandahar airport open so that air combat and transport missions could continue. For the next decade, reserve Seabee battalions were fully integrated into the deployment rotation plan. They also served in Iraq's Anbar Province, where in 2004 Naval Mobile Construction Battalion 14 lost seven members in two separate enemy encounters within a 72-hour period. Reserve Seabees continue to serve in the Central Command area of responsibility today.

Reservists responded in other meaningful ways during the ensuing buildup and execution of Operation Iraqi Freedom. Reserve Navy cargo-handling battalions were instrumental in offloading warfighting sustainment supplies from maritime prepositioning ships in Kuwaiti ports to be processed by other Reserve sailors manning expeditionary customs clearing units and sent to the fight.

Naval Air Force Reserve sailors made significant contributions to Navy efforts in Iraq and Afghanistan:

- Helicopter Combat Support Special Squadrons 4 and 5, whose lineage traces back to the early days of Navy special warfare during the Vietnam era, provided dedicated combat search-and-rescue detachments during Operation Iraqi Freedom. They eventually adapted to a new role as direct support to special-operations forces throughout the 5th Fleet area of responsibility, a mission that re-designated Helicopter Sea Combat Squadron 84 continues today, more than ten years later.

- Fleet Logistics Support Wing squadrons provided 100 percent of the Navy's organic intra-theater airlift, operating from several detachment sites throughout the Middle East.

- Strike Fighter Squadron 201 from Fort Worth, Texas, deployed with Carrier Air Wing 8 on board the USS *Theodore Roosevelt* (CVN-71) from January through May 2003 and participated in Operation Iraqi Freedom combat operations.

- Electronic Attack Squadron 209 executed five expeditionary deployments to Iraq and Afghanistan from 2006 to 2011 before moving from Naval Air Facility Washington, D.C., to Naval Air Station Whidbey Island and transitioning to new EA-18G aircraft.

Since 2001, Navy Reserve medical professionals have made over 5,500 individual deployments providing combat-casualty care at facilities such as the Expeditionary Medical Facility in Kuwait and the NATO Role III Medical Unit in Kandahar. They also manned the Navy Expeditionary Medical Unit at Landstuhl Regional Medical Center in Germany from 2006 to 2014. Other Reserve medical sailors served on extended active duty at Navy medical centers and clinics around the country, some backfilling for deployed active-component personnel.

Sailors have also mobilized as individual augmentees (IAs) to serve in the special-operations community and man deployed joint task forces, specializing in the rule of law, civil affairs, intelligence, logistics, and unmanned aerial systems detachments. Other IAs deployed to man Afghan provincial reconstruction teams and provide security at enemy prisoner-detention facilities. Recently at Camp Lemonnier, Djibouti, more than 60 percent of the camp staff's 289 sailors were Reservists serving in billets across all military occupational specialties, including the camp's senior enlisted leaders and commanding and executive officers. At the same time, approximately 35 percent of Combined Joint Task Force-Horn of Africa headquarters staff was manned by Navy Reserve IAs.

Active-Reserve Integration

The employment of naval combat forces that began in 2001 led to improvements in active-reserve integration and the use of Reserve forces. In 2004 Chief of Naval Operations Admiral Vern Clark directed Fleet Forces Command to perform a zero-based review of all Naval Reserve functions to create a properly integrated and efficiently resourced total force designed to support the Fleet Response Plan. After the review, several thousand reserve billets aligned with Fleet augment units that were either obsolete or unlikely to ever be mobilized were eliminated. To reflect the integration of active and Reserve sailors as one Navy, Admiral Clark asked President Bush to redesignate the U.S. Naval Reserve as the U.S. Navy Reserve in 2005. At the same time, Chief of Navy Reserve

Vice Admiral John Cotton directed that Naval Reserve centers be redesignated as Navy operational support centers to better describe their role in providing trained and ready sailors to support the Fleet. He also directed that active-duty Reserve personnel, known for 50 years as training and readiness of Reserve sailors, be redesignated as full-time support sailors, and ordered their increased integration into Fleet and OPNAV staffs to enhance the Navy's timely access to its Reserve forces.

Whereas the number of Reserve sailors recalled to active duty during the Bosnia and Kosovo conflicts of the 1990s was relatively small, the significant number of Reserve personnel mobilized to support operational commanders after 9/11 proved that the mobilization process, unchanged since the Cold War, needed to evolve. Staffs from OPNAV, the Navy Reserve Force, Bureau of Naval Personnel, and U.S. Fleet Forces Command worked tirelessly to establish mobilization policies and programs to better support Navy Reserve sailors and their families. Initially, sailors were recalled on short notice with only days or weeks to prepare for mobilization. Over time, as the process improved and evolved, sailors were given more advance notice to ready families and employers for deployments, and now receive orders up to 180 days prior to their report date. To prepare for deployment, most IA sailors receive combat skills training at Fort Jackson, South Carolina, or Fort Dix, New Jersey. Since tracking began in 2010, the rate of volunteerism for IA mobilizations has remained consistent at approximately 80 percent, demonstrating the value of a strategic reserve to the total force. Since 9/11, more than 72,000 Reserve sailors have been mobilized to support the Navy, Marine Corps, and joint forces.

Looking Ahead

As the Navy transforms to meet future demands, so too will the Navy Reserve, building on the readiness and operational experience gained over the past decade and a half. As the Navy studies how best to man and train the Fleet to operate new platforms and hardware to meet emerging missions, the Navy Reserve stands ready to support. The 2013 National Defense Authorization Act authorizes involuntary selected Reserve recalls to active duty for preplanned missions in support of the combatant commands. The authority, known as Title 10 U.S. Code 12304b, provides force planners and budget programmers with the means to access Reserve forces for deployment. Currently, U.S. Fleet Forces Command is investigating the utilization of 12304b authority to resource reserve patrol squadron P-3C deployments while Fleet squadrons transition to the P-8A Poseidon aircraft.

Another key area of effort involves developing systems and policies to attract and retain the sailors of the future. The Navy must capitalize on investments in training and readiness of transitioning active-duty personnel by offering opportunities to continue their service as Reserve sailors. A valuable side benefit of a reserve force that serves in communities throughout the country is heightened public awareness of the Navy's vital role in national security, gained through interactions with citizen-sailors.

By aligning with emerging Navy talent-management initiatives, the Navy Reserve will help develop policies that offer sailors the opportunity to transition seamlessly between active and reserve status throughout their careers. Realizing this goal and other visionary efforts requires state-of-the-art pay and personnel systems and policies necessary to maintain force readiness while reducing administrative distractions that can hamper efficiency and negatively affect retention. Robust and agile information technology systems will also allow the Navy to leverage a unique aspect of its Reserve component; Reserve sailors typically possess civilian skills that can be identified and used as a force multiplier. Examples include the boatswain's mate who is a civilian cyber expert, the pilot who flies Boeing 737 (Navy C-40A) aircraft for an airline and serves as an instructor pilot in an air logistics squadron, or the neurosurgeon from the Mayo Clinic who treated nerve-related combat injuries at Landstuhl

Regional Medical Center. Improved technology will allow the Fleet to better use the immense talent base resident in its Reserve component.

This centennial year provides the Navy Reserve with an opportunity to reflect on a century of service to our nation, thank those who have honorably served the force, and pay honor to those Reserve sailors who have selflessly given their lives in defense of our nation and its values. The Navy Reserve will celebrate its rich heritage and legacy as it embarks on its second century of service—providing trained and ready forces to the Navy where and when it matters.

Vice Admiral Braun is the Chief of the Navy Reserve, a position she has held since August 2012. Among her command tours were the Navy Air Logistics Office, Navy Reserve Carrier Strike Group 10 supporting the USS *Harry S. Truman* (CVN-75) and Joint Task Force Katrina, and Tactical Support Center 0793 supporting Patrol and Reconnaissance Wing 5.

2 "Background for the Future of the U.S. Naval Reserve"

James Hessman

U.S. Naval Institute *Proceedings*
(May 1978): 144–57

... UNTIL THE CIVIL WAR, the Navy got along adequately on its own resources. During the Revolution, of course, there was no regular navy. Everyone, in effect, was a reservist. A small regular navy was created during John Adams' presidency, and it conducted very well the small wars with France and the Barbary pirates. In the war of 1812 the Navy had enough officers to man its few ships, but it was not always successful in competing with the privateers for the experienced seamen needed to fill the enlisted ranks. Nonetheless, compared to the Army it felt itself fortunate not to have had to deal with a militia, for the latter had more often been an embarrassment to the nation than an asset. As Captain Reuben Elmore Stivers, U.S. Naval Reserve (Retired), writes in his recently published history of the naval reserve during the country's first century, *Privateers and Volunteers*[1] ". . . with the non volunteer militia units as a horrible example of what not to want, the Navy was careful not to incite such a policy. No one had the slightest idea of how to go about organizing volunteer naval militia units, or what might have been done with them if they had been organized. The Militia Act of 1792 did no more for the Navy than exempt from militia service 'all mariners actually employed in the sea service of any citizen or merchant within the United

States.' The Navy was quite content to let it go at that, and here again we see the emphasis placed on drawing naval manpower in time of war from among men already following the sea as a profession.

But to the Navy's chagrin this procedure did not prove to be as easy as it had been thought to be. When in 1846 Congress authorized an increase in personnel from 7,500 men to 10,000 men for the period of the Mexican War, the Navy was unable to recruit the additional men. At the height of the war—November 1846 to November 1847—not more than 8,000 men served in the Navy at any one time."

Captain Stivers points out that part of the Navy's recruiting problem stemmed from its "reputation and personnel policies," part from the fact that the "Mexican War was fought during a peak period of commercial activity, and the wages of merchant Marine sailors were higher than they had been for several years. Ashore, the average American thought of a war with Mexico as a soldier's war. Clamorous Publicity and patriotic speeches called on men to take up rifle and pack—no one thought much about the Navy's role and the Navy did not speak for itself."

When the Civil War opened in 1861 there were some 1,400 naval officers. Of these, about 300—including many pro-Confederacy—quickly resigned or retired, leaving 1,100: not enough by any means for what was to follow. In consequence some 7,500 volunteer officers were added to the Navy—about as many people as were in all the enlisted ranks at the war's beginning. At first almost all volunteer officers were either former naval officers or masters and mates from the merchant marine (including those whose experience was all on rivers and lakes and who, presumably, were employed by the Navy in similar Waters). But the demand was greater than the supply and eventually about half the Navy's wartime officer Corps came directly from civil life ashore. Promotions for volunteer officers were handled separately from those of the regular navy, but for neither did promotion come easily. In January 1862, for example, there were four rear admirals, 18 commodores, 40 captains, and 91 commanders in the regular navy, and none of any such ranks among the volunteers. Three years later there were among regulars in the same ranks 5, 19, 35, and 67. There was also one full admiral. Of lieutenant commanders, there were 144 in 1862 but only 139 in 1865. Of the volunteers, 13 had risen to the rank of lieutenant commander by 1865. That was it. Everyone else was either in a lower grade or in one of the staff corps (of which, at the time, engineers were by far the largest). Clearly, if one were to advance during the Civil War, neither branch of the Navy, regular or volunteer, was the place to be.

As far as enlisted men went, when the war began the Navy had about 7,600, but many left, according to Captain Stivers, to join the army for they thought "all the action and 'glory' would be found in the infantry, artillery, and cavalry regiments." Others simply deserted. Be that as it may, the enlisted ranks had to be not reduced, but expanded. About 100,000 men did enlist or reenlist though, according to Stivers, "the maximum number of enlisted men in the Navy at any one time" was only about 51,500. At first most of those who joined were former naval seamen, then the number of merchant mariners (including river men) who joined the Navy overwhelmed the number of former naval men, and finally the number of inexperienced "landsmen" overwhelmed them all. When the draft was instituted it was for the Army alone, and it went so far that the Secretary of the Navy complained to Congress that "seamen have been drafted off U.S. Navy ships into the Army . . ." By July 1864 drafted men could enter the Navy if they chose, but by then the war had only nine more months to go.

When the war was over the volunteers were glad to go home and, the evidence suggests, the regulars were glad to let them do so.

For about twenty years after the Civil War the regular navy had all it could do trying to keep some life in its own body. Any interest which might have existed in a reserve naval force remained almost wholly dormant. But, following the naval revival of the 1880s, a number of civilians and naval officers saw the value of some form of reserve force. Massachusetts took the lead, forming a naval militia in 1888, with the governor holding the titles of "Captain General, Commander in Chief, and

Admiral of the land and sea forces of the State."[2] New York was not far behind and eventually quite a number of states had their naval militias. By and large the officers were yachtsmen. The enlisted men might be well-to-do businessmen, or they might be skilled tradesmen. What they certainly were not was professional mariners.

Most militiamen, regular naval officers, and civilian observers saw the main role of the naval militia as a coastal defense force, a few saw them purely as police for riot control work, and another small group viewed them as potential crewmen for short-handed regular fighting ships.

In the event, when war with Spain came in 1898 some 4,000 naval militiamen were released by their governors to federal duty with the Navy. About half of those served in the coastal defense role, some manning Civil War monitors hauled from the mothball fleet of the day. The other half helped man the ships of the fighting fleet off Cuba. At the time the regular navy had about 15,000 officers and men, so the militiamen substantially increased the size of the naval establishment. Some served in otherwise undermanned battleships. Others served in auxiliary cruisers (which were hastily commissioned and armed merchant ships) in which the militiamen provided the entire ship's company save for commanding officer, executive officer, and navigator. Still others served in some of the large steam yachts of the period, such as J. P. Morgan's Corsair which, as the USS *Gloucester*, successfully engaged two Spanish torpedo boat destroyers at the Battle of Santiago.

When the war was over the militiamen went home. The regular navy took to pressing Congress (evidently not too hard) for a federal naval reserve. But the latter did not come to pass, and the State militias continued, with modest support from the regular establishment. Each State naval militia had some ships of its own. In 1913, for example, the California Naval Militia had the use of the small cruiser *Marblehead*; the District of Columbia, the monitor *Ozark* and an armed yacht; Connecticut, the gunboat *Dubuque*; Louisiana, the monitor *Amphitrite* and an armed yacht; Massachusetts, the old cruiser *Chicago* and the torpedo boat *Rodgers*; Maryland, the torpedo boat *Somers*; Michigan, Minnesota,

Missouri, New Jersey, New York, North Carolina, Ohio, Pennsylvania, and Rhode Island, an assortment of ancient gunboats and armed yachts; Oregon, the old cruiser *Boston*; and Washington, the monitor *Cheyenne* and the gunboat *Concord*.

In August 1912 Congress authorized a naval medical reserve corps, a major breakthrough on this front, and in the following year provided for a dental reserve corps. Other laws relating to a national naval reserve followed in quick succession, culminating in the law of 29 August 1916 which formed the Naval Reserve Force. Within a very few months the United States entered World War I (on 6 April 1917) and the regular Navy, which numbered about 60,000 officers and men, was glad, once again, to get all the help it could. The naval militia, mustered in as the National Naval Volunteers, provided over 13,000 officers and men. The Naval Reserve Force, at the beginning hardly more than a name, provided another 330,000 officers and men. When the war ended all elements of the Navy combined totaled about 530,000. Considering the number of regulars on hand when the war began, clearly a large portion of those who enrolled in the regular Navy during the War were regular only in name.

Almost all the Navy's aviation consisted of reservists, including the Navy's only ace, David S. Ingalls. All 12,000 women in the Navy during the war were reservists. Most regular officers and men were assigned to the larger combatants and, in consequence, had no opportunity to participate in anything resembling a battle. The hundreds of submarine chasers, mine layers, minesweepers, supply ships, and trop transports were manned by reservists of one sort or another (though command, wherever possible, reasonably fell to the regulars).

Notes

1. Naval Institute Press, Annapolis; 1975, pp. 173–75. Captain Stivers argues forcefully the view that the privateersmen were the reservists of their day.
2. Kevin R. Hart: "Towards a Citizen Sailor: The History of the Naval Militia Movement, 1888–1898," *American Neptune*, October 1973.

3 "'Let's Get the Yale Gang'"

Rear Admiral Joseph F. Callo, USNR (Ret.)

U.S. Naval Institute *Proceedings*
(September 2001): 64–66

IN 1925, retired Rear Admiral William S. Sims wrote the foreword for the two-volume definitive record—called simply *The First Yale Unit*—of this history-making group. Admiral Sims wrote of one particular member of the group, Naval Reserve Ensign Albert D. Sturtevant, who was the first U.S. military aviator to die in combat in World War I. He described Sturtevant as "a knightly gentleman without fear and without reproach." And although Admiral Sims's description may seem quaintly archaic in today's what's-in-it-for-me world, it was a brilliantly precise description of the men who formed the First Yale Unit, a group driven by ideals of patriotism, courage and selflessness.

The Beginning

The inception of the unit can be traced to 1915, when F. Trubee Davison—then an undergraduate at Yale—traveled to Paris and London with his father, a Wall Street executive. In Europe, Davison got a first-hand view of the war that still was abstract for most Americans. While there, he also spent time driving an ambulance in Paris in the volunteer American Ambulance Field Service. But most important, he had the opportunity to observe the formation of the fabled Lafayette Escadrille and to meet with French pilots who had flown in combat. As a result of the last two circumstances, the idea of becoming a military pilot and forming a squadron to fight in Europe began to take hold in Davison's mind and heart.

On his return for his sophomore year, Davison set about forming a Yale section for the American Ambulance Field Service. The group intended to sail at the end of the school year for Europe, and in June 1916, its members gathered at Gales Ferry, New York. War with Mexico intervened, however, and Davison seized upon the nation's growing attention to military matters as an opportunity to shift his patriotic efforts to his new interest in flying. After discussions with some of his schoolmates, he determined to form a flying unit that would participate in the war in Europe. But first was the matter of parental consent.

To his surprise and delight, he was able to convince his mother his plans were rational; his father was a tougher sell. A telegram to his father, who was in Canada on a fishing vacation, prompted a reportedly discouraging reply: "Have you all gone crazy?" When Davison's father rushed back from Canada, things looked bad, notwithstanding the flyover of a rickety local flying boat staged by Davison to coincide with his father's arrival. But the elder Davison consulted with friends and associates who knew something about the newfangled business of flying; apparently he listened objectively. After a crucial father-and-son boat ride down Long Island Sound to Manhattan, Trubee phoned home: "Father is converted." Both parents eventually became active and important supporters of his efforts to form the flying unit.

Getting off the Ground

Through contacts and with guidance from family and friends, Davison's plans moved forward for the formation of an "Aerial Coast Patrol," an idea gathering momentum among both civilian aviation enthusiasts and the U.S. Navy. At this stage, however, the support of the Navy was guarded. In a letter to Davison dated 14 July 1916 from Secretary of the Navy Josephus Daniels, the Secretary began with the bad news: "[T]here is no provision at the present time whereby the Navy Department can give official recognition to the Aerial Coast Patrol." Then followed the somewhat better news—bureaucratically qualified: "There is, however, provision in the Naval Appropriation Bill . . . for the establishment of a Naval Reserve Flying Corps. . . . You will understand, of course, that the Department cannot give official recognition to persons or organizations over which it has no official control."

Focusing on the positive, Davison pressed on with his efforts to form the unit. The original roster of 12 included himself, Alan W. Ames, Henry P. Davison Jr. (Trubee's younger brother), John V. Farwell III, Artemus L. Gates, Erl C. B. Gould, Robert A. Lovett, Albert D. Sturtevant, John M. Vorys, Charles D. Wiman, Wellesley Laud Brown, and Albert J. Ditman Jr. Only the last two were not Yale men. Then, in 1917, 15 additional Yale men joined the Unit.

During World War I and in postwar years, members of this group distinguished themselves in national service in many ways. For example, the unit produced the only U.S. Navy World War I ace (David Ingalls) and the first U.S. military aviator to lose his life in aerial combat in World War I (Sturtevant). After the war, one became Assistant Secretary of War (Trubee Davison) and another Assistant Secretary of the Navy (Gates). It also produced an Assistant Secretary of War (Lovett) in World War II, a Secretary of Defense (also Lovett), and a four-term member of Congress (Vorys). But for the present, these young men recognized that their country soon would be at war. And especially important, they knew aviation rapidly was becoming a significant element of U.S. military strength.

They accepted the fact that initially they would have to act on their own, and at this point all of the assets and efforts were funded privately. The would-be aviators began their flight training in July 1916 at Port Washington on Long Island Sound with one venerable Curtiss flying boat, nicknamed "Mary Ann," and a civilian instructor named Dave

McCulloch. Later, McCulloch contributed further to the early stages of naval aviation as copilot of the historic NC-3 transatlantic flight. The Mary Ann, which had been donated by Rodman Wanamaker of department store fame, was augmented by two other flying boats, tripling the training assets. One of these had a mahogany hull that gave it more the appearance of a yacht than of a training plane for military pilots. By the end of the summer, four members of the group had soloed, and the others were close to that milestone.

Proving Their Point

In early September 1916, the unit had its first real opportunity to demonstrate its potential military value. The men were asked to carry out two missions as part of the annual training exercise of the Naval Reserve with the active-duty Navy scheduled at Gravesend Bay off Brooklyn. First, they were tasked to locate and report on a simulated minefield that had been laid inside Sandy Hook. Second, they were assigned to locate two destroyers simulating enemy cruisers attempting to get close enough to New York harbor to attack shipping and harbor facilities.

Despite the fact that only one of the two planes that took off on the first mission actually reached the designated area, the unit located, charted, and reported the minefield. After the event, reports indicated the plane that failed to reach the search area had had engine trouble, and Davison, who was piloting the plane, had been forced to make a dead-stick landing in the East River. It also turned out that while waiting for the needed replacement engine part to arrive, the missing crew had enjoyed lunch on board the Davison family yacht, by coincidence moored nearby.

Events associated with the second mission—locating the two "enemy" ships—were even more dramatic. After sighting the two warships, the aircraft involved was returning to make its report when it ran into a severe squall. After a near crash and an emergency landing, the shaken pilot and observer reported their survival—and their ship sighting—by phone. The former did not seem to be of much interest to their colleagues, but the latter was seized upon and reported quickly to the Navy. The two successful missions went a long way toward convincing the Navy of the unit's potential military value, and it became known formally as Volunteer Aerial Coast Patrol No. 1. Although these aviators still were outside the official embrace of the Navy, they were getting closer to military status. Also of great importance, the two successful missions, with progressive embellishment, provided the kind of stories for which Navy aviators have become notorious.

As fall began, the members of the unit returned to their undergraduate work in New Haven, and their training continued on weekends. At this point the group had attracted attention not only for its accomplishments during the Navy's training exercise, but also for stunts such as flying from Port Washington to the Yale campus for Sunday chapel. Fortunately, the university—particularly in the person of Dean Frederick Jones—added its encouragement to the students' voluntary efforts. That encouragement was a noteworthy milestone in Yale's traditional support for its students and graduates serving in the U.S. armed forces—a custom of mutual benefit that came to an inglorious end in the antimilitary convulsions of the 1960s.

In Limbo

In fall 1916, the unit moved its training base to New London, where the would-be pilots worked with the Navy on submarine detection from the air. It was a frustrating time for the band of dedicated volunteers. Everyone agreed that the unit was a good idea, and that it probably would be taken into the Navy as soon as the war began. But the Navy, despite its continued unofficial encouragement, would not provide direct sponsorship. Notwithstanding that inertia, the group continued to gather momentum, as Davison's father, his firm, J. P. Morgan & Co., and friends combined to raise more than $300,000—an astonishing figure at that time—to cover the growing cost of supporting the unit. At the same time,

Yale advanced its support to official endorsement of Davison's and other patriotically motivated students' efforts. The university enlarged its sanction with establishment of a policy that for any "undergraduate in good and regular standing at the time of his leaving, who has advanced into Junior year, due credit towards a degree will be given him for satisfactory work in the Army or Navy."

In early spring, pioneer naval aviator then-Lieutenant John Towers (naval aviator number three), who was in charge of the Navy's aviation desk in Washington, broke the log jam. He recruited the entire unit into the brand-new Naval Reserve Flying Corps, which had been created with congressional appropriations legislation of 1916. With the way cleared by Towers, the group was processed and sworn in at the New London Submarine Base on 24 March, 13 days before the United States entered World War I. Then, on 28 March, the unit left by train for West Palm Beach, Florida, where its members began training full time. Suddenly, The First Yale Unit had made the transition from a few highly motivated college students searching for a way to serve their country in the air, to pioneer members of what became the most powerful naval air arm in the world.

In recording this historic point in his book, *The First Yale Unit*, author Ralph Paine recalled the words of President Abraham Lincoln's Second Inaugural Address: "[W]e dedicate our lives and our fortunes, everything that we are and everything that we have, with the pride of those who know that the day has come when America is privileged to spend her blood and her might for the principles that gave her birth and happiness and the peace which she has treasured."

As the unit advanced in technical proficiency, it also advanced in other important ways. Everyone worked hard and played hard, and what developed was a unique unit esprit de corps, something that has become a cohesive hallmark of U.S. naval aviation. At this point, the unit had made the change from a group of motivated college students to a team of professional military aviators. In the process, they had become a significant part of a rich tradition that spans the years from the earliest experiments in manned flight to space exploration.

It's War

Immediately after the declaration of war, Navy Lieutenant Edward McDonnell—awarded the Medal of Honor for heroism and proficiency at the Battle of Santa Cruz during the Mexican War—was ordered to command the unit. Then, in June 1917, the group was moved, aircraft and all, to a new base at Huntington, Long Island, where the training intensified and the aircraft inventory expanded.

At a time when serious training accidents were an almost routine part of military aviation units, the safety record of The First Yale Unit was exceptional. But in July, Trubee Davison crashed and suffered a broken back. His flying days were over, and he was, in fact, considered lucky to have survived. The unit he had founded, however, was established firmly, and its members rapidly began moving on to positions of leadership in the nation's war effort. In fact, two individuals from the unit were the first members of the Naval Reserve Flying Corps to be ordered to Europe.

Representative of the reputation the unit earned overseas was the comment of one U.S. Navy staff officer in London. He said: "[W]henever we had a member of that Yale Unit, everything was all right. Whenever the French and English asked us to send a couple of our crack men to reinforce a squadron, I would say, 'Let's get some of the Yale gang.' We never made a mistake when we did this."

Post Scripts

Although The First Yale Unit is recognized as the initial volunteer college group to enter the World War I U.S. naval aviation arena, it was by no means the only example of the involvement of U.S. colleges and their undergraduates in the early development of naval aviation. Following the

First Yale Unit closely were such groups as the Aviation Ground School at the Massachusetts Institute of Technology and the 11 Princetonians—including future first U.S. Secretary of Defense James V. Forrestal—who trained with the Canadian Royal Flying Corps in Toronto. There also was a Second Yale Unit, which formed Aerial Coast Patrol Unit No. 2 and trained at Buffalo, New York.

For his personal achievement in establishing The First Yale Unit—recognized as the beginning of the Naval Air Reserve—Davison was awarded the Navy Cross. And in 1966, the 50th anniversary of the Naval Air Reserve, he was designated an Honorary Naval Aviator and awarded his gold wings. It was appropriate recognition for the man whose combination of unselfish patriotism and stubborn dedication to an idea he knew was right was the catalyst for the creation of the Naval Air Reserve.

Admiral Callo was the 1999 *Naval History* magazine Author of the Year. He is the author of *Nelson Speaks* (Annapolis, MD: Naval Institute Press, 2001) and is a Yale man.

4 "The Naval Reserve Officers' Training Corps"

Captain C. W. Nimitz, USN

U.S. Naval Institute *Proceedings*
(June 1928): 441–45

ON MARCH 4, 1925, with the approval of House Resolution 2688, the President set another strong prop under the structure of our national defense. Section 22 of that act authorizes the establishment of a Naval Reserve Officers' Training Corps, the total personnel of which shall not number at any one time more than 1,200. The act confers upon the secretary of the navy powers of control over the Naval R.O.T.C. similar to those exercised by the secretary of war over the Army Reserve Officers' Training Corps which was authorized by the National Defense Act of June 3, 1916, as amended June 4, 1920.

In the Act of March 4, 1925, the term "naval" includes both the Navy and Marine Corps. It was planned by the Navy Department to allot to the Marine Corps one-fifth of the total allowed number of students or 240, and to the Navy four-fifths or 960 students. The Marine Corps has considered, but as yet has not decided to establish separate Marine Corps units, so that for the present, all training has in view the production of efficient naval reserve officers.

Members of the Naval R.O.T.C. are officially known as Naval Reserve Students, and the various undergraduate classes are termed

Naval Reserve Freshmen, Naval Reserve Sophomores, Naval Reserve Juniors, and Naval Reserve Seniors.

In the words of the Navy Department:

> The primary object of the Naval Reserve Officers' Training Corps is to provide systematic instruction and training at civil educational institutions, which will qualify selected students of such institutions for appointment as officers in the Naval Reserve. The Naval Reserve Officers' Training Corps will be expected to supply efficient junior officers to the Naval Reserve and thus assist in meeting the demands for increased commissioned personnel in war time.
>
> The secondary object of the Naval R.O.T.C. is to further acquaint the college authorities and the student bodies with the Navy and what it means to the Nation. The present influence on American public opinion of colleges and universities and the future influence of present day students make this secondary object of considerable importance to the Navy.

Funds for the establishment of naval training units were not made available until the commencement of the fiscal year 1927 (July 1, 1926), for which period Congress appropriated $40,000. With this modest sum the Secretary of the Navy, in the fall of 1926, inaugurated naval units in the following educational institutions: University of California, University of Washington, Harvard, Yale, Georgia School of Technology, and Northwestern University. The administration of these units is conducted by the training division of the Bureau of Navigation under the direction of the chief of bureau. The total allowed personnel under training is equally distributed between the six institutions, and the two hundred naval reserve students at each university are to be further divided between the four undergraduate classes.

Two naval officers and several enlisted men were detailed to each institution in sufficient time to start enrollments upon the opening of the regular fall sessions of 1926. Sixty freshmen from the class of 1930 at each of the selected institutions began their naval experiences simultaneously with their college careers. Naval units will not reach their full authorized strength until the fall of 1929 when that year's allotment of freshmen is enrolled, nor will the system produce naval reserve ensigns before the graduation of the class of 1930 in the spring of that year.

At each of the institutions selected, a four-year course in naval science and tactics, including both theoretical instruction and practical work, has been added to the list of courses offered. During the first two years, students complete a basic course; during the last two years, an advanced course. A cruise of fifteen days at sea in a naval vessel is offered each summer to each naval reserve student, and it is during this time that theoretical instruction gives way to such practical work as boating, marlinspike seamanship, signals, engineering procedure, and navigation. One such cruise is compulsory during the advanced course. All other cruises are voluntary on the part of the students, it being recognized that those students who pay their own way through college must have some of their vacation periods available for remunerative work.

The object of the course in naval science is to supplement the other courses taken at the university so that graduates of both will possess:

(a) A good education.
(b) Sufficient knowledge of such naval subjects as seamanship, navigation, ordnance, military and international law, naval engineering, naval strategy and tactics, and naval communications, to fit them to perform their duties as junior officers of the naval reserve.
(c) A disciplined mind and body.
(d) The quality of self-reliant leadership.

The basic course requires three hours per week and the advanced course five hours per week. The subjects taught in the basic course are navigation, ordnance, and seamanship, to which engineering is added to form the advanced course. Seamanship includes naval regulations, leadership, tactics, and strategy, military and international law; engineering includes mechanical engineering, electrical engineering, and radio. The course in navigation is a complete course in piloting, dead reckoning, nautical astronomy, and compass adjustment, and in addition to fitting the student to perform the duties of a junior officer in the naval reserve will afford the necessary knowledge to pass examinations for papers in the merchant marine. Naval officers of considerable service experience are assigned as instructors. Those institutions having astronomy departments can and do lend valuable aid in the teaching of navigation.

At the University of California, basic course students devote four hours per week to naval work as follows:

Classroom seamanship . . . . one hour
Classroom ordnance and gunnery . . . . one hour
Classroom navigation . . . . one hour
Practical exercises . . . . one hour

Advanced course students will devote an additional hour per week to naval engineering. Practical exercises include infantry drill, boat drill, and gun drill at a four-inch fifty-caliber naval gun mounted on the campus. The above hours are supplemented by occasional visits to ships in port and to the Navy Yard, Mare Island. Students are selected from those who apply with regard to their:

(a) Physical condition.
(b) Latent qualities of leadership.
(c) Probability of attending the university continuously for four years.
(d) Other courses taken at the university.

They must be citizens of the United States, not less than fourteen years of age, and must pass a rigid physical examination prior to acceptance. The physical examination is given by naval medical officers. Only those applicants who are both physically and mentally alert and whose characteristics show that they can be developed into real leaders of men are accepted for enrollment.

The Naval R.O.T.C. forms a natural outlet for those members of Sea Scout organizations who are passing from the high schools into the colleges and universities. These young men usually graduate from a Boy Scout troop into a Sea Scout organization when they are fifteen, and by the time they enter college they have usually spent one or two years learning the rudiments of sea scouting. Because of the limited time available for instruction during the basic course (three hours per week), ex-Sea Scouts who are otherwise mentally and physically qualified, form excellent material for enrollment into the Naval R.O.T.C. Much time will be saved in their preliminary seamanship instruction and they will not be so befuddled on first encountering the nautical phraseology in which our textbooks are written.

Membership in the naval unit does not require any considerable outlay of money on the part of the student. In fact the expense incidental thereto is negligible and is more than offset by the many advantages. Uniforms and textbooks are furnished by the government. The uniforms are similar to those worn by the midshipmen at the U.S. Naval Academy except for the distinctive corps device worn on the sleeve. Advanced course students will be paid a small amount each month, as subsistence allowance while taking the course. This amounts to about $210 for the advanced course, and is the equivalent of a scholarship of that amount given by the Navy Department to each student taking the advanced course. In addition advanced course students will be paid about seventy cents per day while on their summer cruises. Both basic and advanced course students are given subsistence while cruising and are allowed transportation between the university and the port of embarking and debarking from the summer cruises. The university requires a small deposit from each student as a guarantee for the proper care of uniforms and books. This deposit is returned to the student on graduation, or on return of uniform and books in good condition, if withdrawing from the course prior to graduation.

Students who have completed the course will be given a certificate showing such completion. Those who successfully complete the course and graduate from the university will, if recommended by the professor of naval science and tactics, be given a commission as an ensign in the Volunteer Naval Reserve, provided they apply for it. Graduates holding a commission in the Volunteer Naval Reserve and who actively associate themselves with a reserve division and attend drills will become eligible for transfer to the Fleet Reserve. While in the Fleet Reserve and attending regular drills, officers receive yearly a sum equal to two months' active pay in their rank (ensigns about $250). Graduates, however, do not have to remain in the Naval Reserve, and on completion of the course, are not required to accept a commission, but it is believed they will readily see the advantage of so doing.

Those naval units located close to large seaports have a considerable advantage over those less fortunately situated. Visits to ships in port and to adjacent navy yards are frequently arranged during regular sessions to maintain the student's interest and to satisfy the natural desire to see real things pertaining to the sea in addition to studying about them out of books. Occasional opportunities are presented to make short cruises or underway visits to ships of the fleet. On the West Coast the U.S.S. *Tennessee*, one of the largest and latest of battleships, was designated to make the cruise during the summer of 1927 for the naval units of the University of California and the University of Washington. During the summer of 1928 the U.S.S. *Pennsylvania* will take about fifty members of University of California naval unit to Victoria, B.C., in time to participate in the celebration of Empire Day and Victoria Day.

Naval Reserve students are admitted to the advanced course only on their written application and agreement to continue training in the advanced course until the completion thereof, unless sooner discharged. They further agree in writing to attend one advanced cruise. In return for the additional work required during the advanced course, the government pays the student a total of approximately $225 in cash and furnishes him with subsistence while on cruise.

Is this contract mutually advantageous to the student and to the government? From the student's standpoint it certainly should appear so. First of all, in the so-called "Land grant institutions" military or naval training is compulsory for the first two years, during which time he must complete a basic course. While he receives no pay from the government during this preliminary period, he will, if in the Naval R.O.T.C. unit, receive a well-fitting tailored uniform made of excellent material which he can wear to social functions as well as to drills and recitations. He also has the opportunity of making visits of inspection to various types of naval vessels, and during his summer vacation he can make a two weeks' cruise on a man-of-war during which his expenses will be practically nil. How many boys dream of cruising on a man-of-war and how few are accorded the privilege!

During his second two years in college the monthly commuted ration check from Uncle Sam will help to meet many small bills in case he is hard pressed financially, or to furnish small luxuries if he has just enough money to get him through college with nothing left over for frills. And the work required to earn this check is interesting even though it requires five hours per week. By that time the student will have learned how to get the most study out of the available time—something which he usually does not know on entering college—and will be in a position to devote five hours to Uncle Sam's course in addition to the time required for his regular work.

And on graduation, in addition to receiving his diploma and a degree, he may, if he so elects, receive a commission as an ensign in the U.S. Naval Reserve. If he continues, as he should and probably will, to maintain an active interest in naval affairs, and if he joins a fleet reserve division soon after graduation, he will keep in line of promotion and will have the satisfaction of knowing that he is carrying his share of the burden and duty of national defense. Furthermore, while actually serving in the Fleet Naval Reserve and attending regular drills, he will be receiving each year from the government two months' pay which represents a sum not to be lightly regarded in starting life's rocky road.

What a satisfaction it will be for him to know, that in the emergency of war, he can jump immediately into a station previously assigned, a station for which he has trained and in which he can render useful service. Contrast his frame of mind with that of the graduate who, though patriotic enough, took only the minimum required military or naval training while at college, and who, since graduation has been interested only in his business. The emergency of war will probably find him bewildered as to what he can or should do, and if he does not do something voluntary at once, he will soon have his mind made up for him by some form of conscription. This may be the easiest way for him, but is he giving the government the best that should be expected of a college graduate?

Now let us examine the contract from the government's standpoint. It is estimated that the total cost of the equipment to be furnished to the six selected institutions will be $60,000. As this sum is to be expended over a period of four years, the average cost per year for material will be $15,000, but this will be for the first four years only. After that the yearly expenditure for material will be much reduced, as it need cover only the normal wear and tear, with occasional additional sums for new items of equipment.

The cost of training per student at the University of California can be roughly estimated as follows:

(a) First uniform outfit (basic course) $55
(b) Second uniform outfit (advanced course)........$50
(c) Three summer cruises (transportation,
     subsistence, and pay) $70
(d) Advanced course—commutation of rations.... $315
(e) Miscellaneous transportation $10
     Total... $500

Suppose at the end of ten years the system were suddenly shut down. What will be the cost to the government per graduate? By that time seven classes will have graduated. Assuming a maximum total of 240 graduates per year from all six institutions we can expect 1,680 to have been commissioned. Costs will be approximately as follows:

(a) Original equipment—spread over first
four years..................................$60,000
(b) Wear and tear and replacement of lost or
damaged equipment, five per cent per year,
commencing at end of first year............$27,000
(c) 1,680 graduates at $500 per graduate.....$840,000
(d) 360 freshmen on each of whom
$55 has been spent.........................$19,800
(e) 300 sophomores on each of whom
$75 has been spent.........................$22,500
(f) 240 juniors on each of whom
$275 has been spent........................$66,000
(g) Pay of enlisted men attached to naval unit
(in excess of retired pay) $242,000
Total for 1,680 graduates $1,277,300
Cost per graduate $760

If, however, the system continues, and it is reasonable to expect that it will continue, items (d), (e) and (f) can be omitted, making the total cost per graduate approximately $700. These estimates do not include the cost of maintenance of cruising nor the salaries of naval officers acting as instructors or administrators of the Naval R.O.T.C., which items are a part of the fixed charges which the government normally bears, irrespective of the existence of the Naval R.O.T.C. Nor has the interest on the investment been included. The cost does include the excess of active pay over retired pay of three retired chief petty officers who are on duty with each naval unit.

While the approximate cost per graduate can be roughly determined, it is a great deal more difficult to determine each graduate's value to the government. There are too many intangible factors to be evaluated. In addition to the graduate's increased value as a trained reserve officer prepared to step into an important position in the naval scheme for naval defense in time of war, is his increased value as a citizen. We can expect him to be a strong supporter of internal law and order, and of any movement to keep the armed forces of the country in a "reasonably defensive posture"; and, in so far as the Navy is concerned, we may be sure that in his daily mingling with his business associates, he will preach the gospel of a Navy second to none.

And in the growth and upbuilding of a merchant marine we will find in each graduate a firm advocate. There will be some who, by reason of their liking of the sea and their acquisition of the requisite technical knowledge, will find their careers in the merchant marine. And where will we find better personnel to carry our goods around the world than our naval trained college graduates who elect to follow that line of endeavor? The growth of our merchant marine need not be delayed by reason of lack of trained officer personnel.

The graduates of the Naval Reserve Officers' Training Corps units will be young men of great energy, strong determination, and high character, because it will take just those qualities to make the college student accept the extra workload and see it through. Naval Academy graduates do not soon forget the steady grind of four years at Annapolis. During each academic year of eight months a midshipman devotes about seventeen hours each week to classroom recitations. During a similar period of each year, naval reserve students must spend approximately the same number of hours on recitations and lectures, and in addition, the three or five hours per week on naval subjects.

At the University of California about seventy-five per cent of the students work their way through, either wholly or in part, and the naval unit has its proportion of this type of student. Remunerative employment ranges all the way from three to eight hours per day during the regular session, to steady employment during vacations. A bureau of occupations at the university assists students to find the type of work they are capable of doing. Students are employed as clerks, ushers, actors, janitors, watchmen, bakers, cooks, waiters, tutors, drivers, gardeners, conductors, brakemen, gatemen, oil station employees, laundry workers, stevedores, salesmen, and in many other capacities. One student owns his own concrete mixer with which he does odd jobs to see him through. Truly he is making his way via a hard route.

Roughly speaking, the time spent by a midshipman in practical work must be spent by the average student in remunerative employment, with this difference—the midshipman usually need not worry about the allocation of his time. That is done for him. Not so with the naval reserve student who must work. He must frequently hunt for his employment. Those students who go out for athletics, that is, the varsity teams, carry an additional load.

Has the government made a wise investment in the establishment of the Naval R.O.T.C.? We think that in the passage of time this question will be answered in the affirmative.

5

"Notes on U.S. Naval Reserve Aviation"

Lieutenant Commander J. B. Lynch, A-O, USNR

U.S. Naval Institute *Proceedings*
(April 1939): 473–86

ALTHOUGH THE U.S. NAVAL RESERVE is by law a component part of the U.S. Navy, and during the World War comprised a large percentage of the total personnel of the Navy, relatively few officers of the regular service are familiar with its composition, organization, and the abilities of its personnel. However, since July, 1936, when aviation cadets began to come out of Pensacola in large numbers and report to their assignments with the Aeronautic Organization of the Fleet, the Navy as a whole has become more conscious of the Naval Reserve and particularly of its aviation branch.

The intent of this article is to review briefly the history of Naval Reserve Aviation, beginning in 1916 with the enactment of legislation in anticipation of the possible entry of the United States into the World War; thence through the wartime expansion, demobilization, and practical extinction of the Naval Reserve in 1921; the meager beginnings of its rehabilitation commencing in 1923; and the relatively slow but steady progress up to the commencement of the aviation cadet Program in 1935. Brief comment will be made on the aviation cadet program itself, its reason for being, the measure of success it has met, and its resultant product, an aviation reserve which will be unquestionably the finest possessed by any of the world naval powers. It is believed that the service as a whole is interested to know what will become of the aviation cadets, so far as their naval reserve connections are concerned, after they have completed their four years of service with the Navy; what provisions have been made to maintain their efficiency as naval aviators and to keep them ready for immediate mobilization in time of war or national emergency.

Public Act No. 241, 64th Congress, entitled "An Act making appropriations for the Naval Service for the fiscal year ending June thirtieth, nineteen hundred and seventeen, and for other purposes" as approved August 29, 1916, included as a rider a provision for the establishment of the Naval Reserve Flying Corps. This legislation laid the groundwork for the tremendous personnel expansion of the Navy which followed the entry of the United States into the World War.

In April, 1917, there were on active duty in the Naval Flying Corps 38 officers designated as naval aviators and 163 enlisted men in aviation ratings. On November 11, 1918, there were 1,856 naval aviators, 288 officers designated as student naval aviators, 391 ground officers, and 3,881 students under training for commissions. There were 21,951 enlisted men in aviation ratings, and 8,742 general ratings assigned to aviation, making a total enlisted personnel of 30,693 and a total personnel of 36,909. Most of this expansion was accomplished by means of the Naval Reserve.

Shortly after the signing of the Armistice the demobilization of the Naval Reserve Flying Corps set in with the return of personnel to civil life, and by 1920 only a small group of reserve officers remained on active duty. Most of these soon took examinations for the regular Navy and by 1923 the Naval Reserve Flying Corps was completely inactive.

In 1920, funds were provided for 15-day training duty periods for a limited number of reserve officers. However, owing to lack of funds for the purpose, this opportunity was not again offered, and subsequently all naval reserve aviators remaining on the rolls were transferred to the inactive Class 6 of the Volunteer Naval Reserve Force. Without the incentive of actual flying, hundreds of aviation reserve officers failed to re-enroll at the expiration of their first 4 years of service and passed out of the Naval Reserve Flying Corps.

In November, 1922, the Bureau of Aeronautics recommended to the Secretary of the Navy a policy designed to foster and maintain an efficient Naval Aviation Reserve. The interest in flying of hundreds of reserve officers, as indicated by their letters to the Department, was recognized, and it was desired to take advantage of this interest in the formation of an active Naval Aviation Reserve. A short time later the Navy Department supplied the Fifth Division of the Sixth Battalion, New York Aerial Police, with four N9 training seaplanes. The unit had its base located at Fort Hamilton, New York, and was supported partly by the subscriptions of wealthy individuals. Those members of the aerial police authorized to fly in naval aircraft were required to be members of the Naval Reserve Force.

In April of the following year, the Bureau of Aeronautics recommended for the consideration of the Chief of Naval Operations a definite reserve aviation policy. This proposed the establishment of a number of reserve aviation bases throughout the country, the reenrollment of desirable former naval reserve aviators, provision of funds for annual training periods, and the training of a certain number of student aviators each year. By the summer of 1923, reserve aviation units were actually established at Fort Hamilton, New York, Squantum, Massachusetts, and Great Lakes, Illinois. These units were provided with aircraft and material, funds for maintenance, and reserve officer and enlisted personnel on permanent active duty. The mission was defined as the enrollment and training of new members sufficiently young and suitable officer material, insuring a supply of new blood, and the maintenance of efficiency of members already qualified. In the summer of 1923, 33 students were enlisted as seamen, second class, and given 45 days of preliminary training duty at Squantum and at Fort Hamilton. During the following summer they were given 45 days of advanced training at the Naval Air Station, Hampton Roads, Virginia, and at the conclusion examined professionally, those found qualified being commissioned as ensigns, Class 5, U.S.N.R.F.

On March 24, 1926, largely as a result of the report of the President's Aircraft Board (known as the Morrow Board) and the Selected Committee of Inquiry into Operation of the United States Air Services (H.R., 68th Congress, known as the Lampert Committee), the Navy Department adopted a 5-year program for training the Aviation Reserve. This had at first been proposed as legislation, but finally was adopted as a Navy Department policy. It was designed to provide personnel for the minimum naval reserve aviation force which would be required at the outbreak of hostilities. Up to this time, practically no provision had been made for the training of naval reserve enlisted men. In accordance with a new policy, organized reserve aviation divisions and squadrons were established in various sections of the country, with definite authorized complements of officers and enlisted men. They conducted weekly drills and underwent 15-day annual training periods, and each division was accorded a definite place and mission in the War Plans.

In the fiscal year 1928 the naval reserve appropriation for the first time provided funds for training duty for one year in the aircraft squadrons of the U.S. Fleet for 50 naval reserve aviators of the rank of ensign. The performance of flight duties of these individuals in fleet assignments brought glaringly to light the inadequacy of their basic flight training. Accordingly, it was decided to give all student aviators of the Naval Reserve the full naval flight training and ground school course at Pensacola. Since 1929 the advanced flight training of all naval reservists has been conducted at Pensacola, the personnel being assigned in classes with the regular officer students and taking the full course prescribed by the Bureau of Navigation for designation as a naval aviator.

Until the commencement of the aviation cadet program in 1935, all reserve student aviators underwent training at Pensacola in the rating of seamen, second class. Upon completion of the course, they were commissioned as ensigns in the Naval Reserve, and, subject to their own consent, assigned to active duty for training with fleet aviation squadrons for one year. Upon the conclusion of the period of fleet duty, they were released from active duty and, where practicable, became associated with naval reserve aviation squadrons at naval reserve aviation bases. Beginning with the fiscal year 1930, the progress and increase of efficiency of naval reserve aviation became very marked. This was attributable largely to:

(1) The high standards governing the selection of candidates

(2) The excellence of the basic training at Pensacola which gave reserve officers the same flight training as officers of the regular Navy

(3) The year of active duty with the U.S. Fleet

(4) The provision of advanced service type aircraft for reserve aviation squadrons for the maintenance of efficiency

(5) Consolidated drill periods for aviation squadrons

(6) Establishment of annual flight syllabus of training for reserve aviators

(7) Competition among squadrons and among reserve aviation bases for rating in relative efficiency, as determined by marks assigned by the Naval Reserve Inspection Board

With the building up of the Navy to treaty strength and the accompanying expansion of the peace-time aeronautic organization of the regular Navy to almost twice its previous size, there resulted a greatly increased requirement for pilots. Owing to increased requirements for line officers in the Navy as a whole, and other considerations, it was not possible to meet pilot needs by the training of additional officer pilots of the regular service. The Navy Department desired and proposed to solve the problem by training annually at Pensacola a greatly increased number of Naval Reservists and extending the period of active duty with the fleet from one to three years. This plan met with objections on the grounds of expense by the Bureau of the Budget, which suggested the training of an increased number of enlisted pilots to meet requirements, a solution which was not acceptable to the Navy Department on the grounds of policy. The aviation cadet program was adopted as a compromise between the two.[1]

The grade of aviation cadet in the Naval Reserve was created by Public Act No. 37, 74th Congress, approved April 15, 1935. Since that time, 1,987 young college men who have been found educationally, morally, physically, and psychologically qualified, have been enlisted as seamen, second class, and given elimination flight training at naval reserve aviation bases. Of this number, 1,450 have been selected for further training, appointed as aviation cadets, and ordered to active duty undergoing training at Pensacola; 719 have successfully completed the training, being designated as naval aviators, and ordered to active duty with the Aeronautic Organization of the U.S. Fleet; 300 are now at Pensacola undergoing training; over 1,000 are on the active duty rolls.

The standards for original selection are exceptionally exacting. Those selected are the best of thousands of young college men throughout the country who apply each year for the training.[2] The rigid requirements of the training insure that only those with the highest demonstrated officer qualifications complete successfully and are ordered to the fleet. During the 3-year period of duty with the fleet, the duty performed by the aviation cadets is in all respects that of qualified commissioned officers. As a group, the aviation cadets have made a decidedly favorable impression in the fleet, and have carried out their assigned duties in a most satisfactory manner.

It seems desirable to comment on the fatal accident rate for aviation cadets as compared with pilots of the regular service, as in many quarters there is an impression that the aviation cadet accident rate is relatively and unduly high. The records of the Department show that since the inception of the program, 23 aviation cadets have been killed while serving on active duty after graduation from Pensacola. Of these, only 13 lost their lives while acting as pilots. During this period, there have been 48 fatal accidents in the fleet aeronautic organization in which 35 of the actual pilots were other than aviation cadets.

Tabulated by fiscal year:

Fiscal Year	Fatal Accidents	Aviation Cadet Pilots
1937	14	2
1938	20	6
1939 (to 30 Dec.)	14	5
	—	—
	48	13

While the number of pilots of the regular service in the fleet aeronautic organization has been considerably in excess of the number of aviation cadets so assigned, particularly in the first and second years of the program, it will be seen that the foregoing figures do not reflect unfavorably upon the aviation cadets.

The question is frequently asked how long will the Navy find it necessary to use aviation cadets, or stated differently, when will it be possible to meet requirements through the training as aviators of a sufficient number of officers who are graduates of the Naval Academy. The answer is that on the basis of four appointments to the Naval Academy per congressman there will probably never be sufficient officers in the Navy to meet the requirements for officer pilots, based on the treaty navy (1,910 airplanes) program. In the event that the 3,000-airplane program authorized by the Walsh-Vinson Bill in the 75th Congress becomes an actuality, the possibility of meeting requirements from present regular navy sources will become even more remote. The Navy Department now considers that this is a desirable situation since the introduction of a large number of short service pilots in the grade of aviation cadet not only contributes to a rapid building up of a highly efficient and well-trained Naval Reserve, but greatly reduces the base of the pyramid of promotion of commissioned officers required otherwise to be in the regular Navy, and so reduces the percentage of forced attrition in the higher ranks.

Beginning in July, 1939, and continuing monthly thereafter, groups of aviation cadets will complete their 4-year periods of service and be returned to civil life, their places in fleet assignments being taken by newly graduated aviation cadets coming out of Pensacola. Each of them will receive $1,500 in cash, in addition to any pay and allowances to which he may otherwise be entitled, for the purpose of tiding him over the period of getting established in civil life. All will become eligible for commissions in the Naval Reserve with dates of rank as of dates of appointments as aviation cadets. Those who live in the general vicinities of reserve aviation bases will be assigned to aviation squadrons of the Organized Reserve and expected to maintain their efficiency by the performance of regular drills and annual training duty. Those residing at remote points, or who for business or other reasons are unable to affiliate with the Organized Reserve, will be assigned to the Volunteer Reserve.

The Navy now maintains naval reserve aviation bases at Boston, New York, Philadelphia, Washington, D.C., Miami, Detroit, Chicago, Minneapolis, Saint Louis, Kansas City, Long Beach, Oakland, Calif., and Seattle. The principal functions of these bases are:

(1) To provide facilities for the training and maintenance of efficiency of the officers and enlisted men of the aviation branch of the Naval Reserve.

(2) To conduct elimination flight training of selected candidates for appointments as aviation cadets in the Naval Reserve and the Marine Corps Reserve.

All of these bases are equipped to perform their own overhaul and maintenance of aircraft and engines, and actually perform this work as a part of the training for reservists, the quality of their work being in every way up to the high standard set by the overhaul centers of the regular establishment. All of the permanent personnel at the bases are reservists excepting the commanding officers, who in most cases, and as a matter of policy, are naval aviators of the regular Navy. These commanding officers come directly to the reserve aviation bases from fleet aviation duties, and so bring to the Naval Reserve the benefit of recent fleet experience. In addition to their command duties, they are responsible for the supervision of instruction of the reserve aviation squadrons attached.

Affiliated with all naval reserve aviation bases are naval reserve aviation squadrons whose peace-time organization, so far as practicable, is based upon that of a scouting squadron of the regular service. The squadron organization provides for 23 flight officers, 1 medical officer, 1 supply officer, and 66 enlisted men in appropriate ratings. The assigned aircraft are modern high performance service types identical with or similar to types in use in the fleet.

During the course of each fiscal year, all squadrons of the Organized Reserve are required to perform not less than 48 drill periods for which pay is received, and to perform not less than 14 days annual training duty with pay. The officers are required to complete an annual syllabus of flying prescribed by the Bureau of Navigation, which comprises gunnery, bombing, tactical flying, navigational flying, instrument flying, night flying, extended flying, carrier landing practice, and communication training. The methods of scoring in record gunnery and bombing practices and the procedure in other phases of the syllabus are based upon current practices in fleet aviation. The enlisted men in aviation ratings perform appropriate work in connection with the operation and maintenance of the aircraft and attend classes to increase their efficiency and prepare them for advancement, the yeomen and other non-aviation ratings also performing work and receiving training appropriate to their ratings.

The aviation branch of the Organized Naval Reserve is unique in many respects. Since the educational and other standards for selection for the training are very high, the basic nonprofessional qualifications of the officer personnel compare favorably with those of graduates of the Naval Academy. When to this is added the full naval flight training course for officers of the regular service, and from one year to three years with the fleet (depending upon the time at which the officer qualified), it will be seen that the professional qualifications of the reserve aviators, as a group, are superior to those of any other class of the Naval Reserve. The reserve aviators are proud of their naval training, background, and tradition. Their morale is exceptionally high. They are thoroughly trained military pilots who maintain their flying efficiency in the most modern, high performance service type aircraft. They are kept abreast of the latest developments in fleet aviation by the system of assignment of regular officers to command the reserve aviation bases, and by the influx to the squadrons of newly commissioned reserve officers fresh from long periods of active duty with the aviation forces afloat. Although no new officers have come into the organized squadrons from the fleet since July 1, 1936, due to the 4-year requirement for service for aviation cadets, there will be a steady influx commencing with the release from active duty in July, 1939, and commissioning of the first group of aviation cadets who commenced training at Pensacola in July, 1935. Naval Reserve Aviation, with approximately 100 officers on active duty as instructors at Pensacola and more than 1,000 aviation cadets in service, takes pride in the knowledge that even in time of peace it provides a most important and indispensable part of the aeronautic organization of the Navy.

Notes
1. It is interesting to note that the Congress increased from $5,000 to $10,000 the life insurance policy for aviation cadets upon which the premiums are paid by the government; and increased to $1,500 the cash payment to aviation cadets upon release from active duty after 4 years of service. As a result, the net cost to the government at the end

of the 4-year period is not materially less than would have been the case had these individuals been commissioned as ensigns upon completion at Pensacola, assuming that they remained unmarried during their three years of active duty with the fleet.

2. Represented in the present aviation cadet body are all the states in the Union and more than 350 accredited colleges.

"The Corn Belt Navy"

6

Lieutenant Ralph C. Lowes Jr., DE-O, USNR

U.S. Naval Institute *Proceedings*
(April 1939): 473–86

IT IS A LONG DISTANCE from salt water to the heart of the Corn Belt and yet, curiously enough, situated in the center of this strictly agricultural area we find the United States Navy formally represented by established units of its Organized Reserve. The local development and administration of these units furnishes a unique chapter in the history of the modern service as a whole and an enlightening testimonial to the unusually high degree of assimilation and creative genius which can be developed by the inherent yearning of the landlubber for the sea. This brief is in no way intended to be offered as a manual of administration for naval reserve units but only as a recital of certain problems which confront an inland division and the apparent solutions thereto, together with the writer's observations extending over 15 years of intimate association with the Reserve.

The evolution of the Naval Reserve from the era of its swaddling clothes to its current progressive status reveals a most interesting story of problems met in practically every instance by the good old trial-and-error method. It was learned early in its existence there was no rule-of-thumb procedure for the attainment of a given objective. Each group was confronted with conditions peculiar to its particular locality which it must successfully overcome to arrive in time at the same ultimate goal. That this goal, which is rather specifically defined as that status of the organization which will provide the maximum utility to the regular Navy in time of an emergency, is of somewhat uncertain limits, has been evidenced by the frequent modification of policy on the part of the administrative head, the regular Navy. Thus local administration must be versatile as well as progressive. The writer's reactions are, of course, entirely personal and as set down here will, no doubt, be differed with now as they have been in the past by colleagues in similar capacities in adjacent communities. However, the following paragraphs endeavor to set forth the major problems which confront the Inland Reserve and the course pursued, or indicated to be pursued, in meeting them.

The officer personnel factor continues to be the paramount consideration. The allowed quota in an Organized Reserve Division comprises four line, one medical, and one supply officer. This number, however, is not believed to be sufficient to properly carry out Armory Schedules and, therefore, it is considered advisable to have attached additional volunteer line officers. These additional volunteer officers also serve to improve the efficiency of the officer group as a whole because organized officers will strive to do a better job to justify their retention in that select classification and volunteers will similarly put forth their best efforts to endeavor to qualify for an organized vacancy, if and when it should occur. That the selection of commissioned officers is of greatest importance is obvious. In Middle West communities there is naturally a smaller potential group of persons otherwise qualified by virtue of educational, economic, and social background who have elementary naval experience. The natural sources are, therefore, in the order named: Naval Academy graduates, Naval R.O.T.C. graduates, reserve enlisted personnel, and interested civilians. Experience has shown that the mere fact that the prospective officer is a Naval Academy graduate is not, in itself, supporting proof he will be a positive adjunct to the division. Occasional cases have presented themselves where an attitude of benevolent superiority was apparent. Unbelievably, this type of Academy graduate indicates that he will condescend to offer his services to your lowly group and thereby elevate its efficiency and prestige by his unselfish contributions. It goes without saying that the inclusion of such an officer into the Division Organization would have a devastating effect on morale. Fortunately, a preliminary discussion with the prospective applicant will obviate such a possibility and the right type of Naval Academy graduate remains the No. 1 candidate. Most Naval R.O.T.C. graduates are, of course, highly desirable. The commissioning of enlisted personnel, as always, is fraught with danger. The greatest care must be exercised that a good petty officer isn't lost by his becoming a miserable commissioned officer and that we don't find ourselves ending up with a slight distortion of the old bromide, "You can take the man out of the foc'sle but you can't take the foc'sle out of the man." Manifestly, selection of commissioned officers from strictly civilian status requires the most careful selection combined with the confirmed obligation on the commanding officer's part to proper training, instruction, and indoctrination. Thus, in summarizing this all-important phase of reserve administration, and made proportionately more difficult because of the reduced number of potential candidates, the selection and retention of the commissioned personnel to insure competent, loyal, and enthusiastic participation remains the paramount issue.

A review of the historical background of most of the Inland Reserve Divisions will disclose that the nucleus for the establishment of the various units was originally an organization of State Naval Militia which, upon declaration of war in 1917, transferred to the Navy and which, upon demobilization, sought to reestablish their entities. This was the situation the writer found when he presented himself to take command of such a group in September, 1923. This particular unit had, through the 4 neglected years following the war, dwindled to but 9 men, but what was lacking in numbers was, fortunately, offset by individual enthusiasm and the fact they represented an experienced, above-average group. It is interesting to note of that original 9, 5 are still active leaders in the division. To this small number fell the problem of recruiting and, as it happened, due to the fact that like attracts like, the very finest type was presented for enlistment from this source. To them it was a club with their war service as a point of common interest. Attributable, no doubt, to the desire for necessary rapid expansion, an early mistake of enlisting several lads who didn't fit in taught the first lesson in selection. It threatened the structure and existence of the whole organization and, therefore, it was thereafter decreed that recruits would only be acceptable after a vote of approval of active members. This one all-important factor, initial selection, seems to be the answer to many of the problems now confronting divisions and erroneously disguised under other classifications. Gradually new procurement and acceptance methods were devised and employed until today it is believed a practical and satisfactory solution has been found; at least, it is felt the ultimate in recruiting has been attained, namely, a waiting list. All candidates are vouched for by a member or are believed to possess the necessary qualifications by personal knowledge. Many of the members are sons of men who are personally known to the commanding officer and who requested that their boys be enlisted. Every candidate is first interviewed and informed of his obligation in detail. This includes a definite commitment from him of his intention to attend drills regularly and to cruise with the division. He is then required to take the regular Navy O'Rourke General Classification Test, under the supervision of the supply officer who has the required time to devote to this feature on drill nights, and to attain a grade of 70 per cent. The value of this to improved efficiency cannot be underestimated. When its use was decided upon, it was tested by requiring every active member of the division to submit to it and the results were remarkably true in defining the value of the individual to the division. That is, those members who made the lowest grades were distinctly those members who consistently lowered the merit at annual inspection. Then, too, an individual case is a sad memory. One likely candidate had made only a 53 per cent on his I.Q. and was informed of his failure to qualify. Shortly thereafter a committee of members presented themselves and requested that this requirement be waived because he was expected to be a valuable adjunct to the division baseball team. In a weak moment permission was granted to go ahead and enlist him. Baseball season ended and so did his interest but equally important was the fact that his whole period of active participation in division work was marked by an inability to assimilate instruction and throughout his entire tenure of membership he represented a distinct detriment. His removal and subsequent substitution operated against the turnover factor and he had kept out a good man in the interim. The officers are sold 100 per cent on the use of the I.Q. and so is the division.

This particular unit's recruiting area comprises a population of approximately 150,000; however, only three members of the division reside outside the city. These three drive 40 miles to drill but the very fact they are at drill every week regardless of rain, sleet, or blizzard constitutes, it is believed, an example to the rest of the division whose problem under such conditions is much less acute. Care is taken not to recruit too many from one business establishment. There is the natural tendency to bring in the buddy from the next desk or bench. However, when cruising time comes, the employer, who is usually willing and eager to cooperate, quite naturally cannot and will not suffer a disruption of his organization through leaves of absence to too great a proportion of his personnel.

That phase of division administration which, of course, offers the widest range of initiative and the greatest diversification of policy lies in the extracurriculum activities. No effort will be made to include a discussion of professional training methods since this is a more or less standardized procedure and will be common to all reserve units. But practice has taught us that what may be termed extracurriculum activities are potent stabilizing and morale building elements. The usual representative athletic teams have been given trials. Our experience leads definitely to the conclusion that if the teams' personnel is developed normally from the ranks of the division, excellent; but if the emphasis is on the team and the recruiting primarily with that in mind, the percentage of good to be gained is distressingly low. In fact, experience leads to the definite conclusion it just won't work. However, representative rifle, baseball, basketball, and bowling teams are supported with results successful enough to warrant continuance, although intra-divisional contests seem to give better results and so deck force–engineer contests are enthusiastically endorsed and received.

The value of appeal to individual effort and suitable reward is, however, recognized. Seven years ago was instituted the "Most Valuable Reservist" award. The factors used in determining this annual award were set up in accordance with the following table and as yet no reason has been found to modify them or their values.

Rules: (1) Competition to commence July 1 and terminate June 30

       (2) Eligibility for award—mandatory

          (a) Perform annual training duty with division

          (b) Be present at annual inspection

Multiple—weight   A-GENERAL

50   20   (1) Drill attendance

      10   (2) Military bearing and man-o'-war's man appearance

       5   (3) Week-end cruises or equivalent interest in subchaser

       5   (4) Interest in division activities

      10   (5) Co-operation and general demeanor

             B-PROFICIENCY IN RATING

50   20   (1) Training course work

      20   (2) Practical ability

      10   (3) Leadership

Every member, rated or nonrated, is eligible and has an equal opportunity to attain it. An engraved certificate is presented with appropriate ceremony and the event, through the press, is given widespread publicity throughout the community. A pronounced individual effort to its attainment is apparent. The division officers acting as an award committee select the recipient. All are definitely sold on both its psychological and practical value as potent factor for division improvement.

Six years ago the publication of a monthly division paper was commenced. From a modest beginning this has grown into an excellent editorial effort. The staff is composed entirely of enlisted personnel and great interest is manifested in its preparation and equally great is the anticipation of the membership of the division on its date of issue. Besides offering a splendid vehicle for the dissemination of pertinent information to the membership of the unit it tends to bring about a closer contact with the individual member's family and friends when it finds a resting place on the magazine rack at home. In addition, it is accepted and placed on the reading racks of the public libraries and thus directly operates as a public prestige-building element. The extent of the present mailing list, composed of interested persons throughout the entire country and on ships at sea who have individually requested it, testifies completely to its excellence and value. Its cost is a nominal one borne by the division "kitty."

Reference to the family of the member brings out the matter of the immeasurable good to be derived from appropriate handling of that significant factor. The chief source of difficulty in gaining cruise and drill attendance can be traced to family opposition, either direct or indirect. This resistance is not at all unnatural. The family is naturally reluctant to approve the man's taking the two weeks allotted to their summer vacation with a cruise on the cool lake waters while they remain at home and swelter in the throes of Corn Belt summer temperatures, and this, remember, in almost every car with the regular income materially reduced to navy pay schedules. Regular absence in the evening for drill attendance, while not so provoking and certainly more remunerative, still is a feature not to be overlooked. Again experience tells us that we definitely must find a way to compete with the family attitude. Our solution is to include the family in every division activity practicable. Picnics, dances at the armory, etc., are arranged and enthusiastically supported. Each year a Navy Day banquet of a rather pretentious nature is arranged, all this to include the family. Flowers are sent to reservists or members of their family when ill. We must, we feel, make that member's family a part of the division and, therefore, a positive gesture to the family is an enterprise which will pay dividends in improved division efficiency, as well as, it might be added, better and more enthusiastic care and upkeep of those uniforms.

The unit is frequently enlisted to participate in civic functions such as parades, dedications, receptions, funerals, etc. Attendance at all such functions is made entirely voluntary and the definite understanding is given that authorized drill and annual cruises are the only mandatory attendance requirements. The employment of the uniformed Naval Reservist to add color to an occasion is a common request but it was learned a long while ago that it is almost an impossibility to discriminate between the value of individual requests and not offend. However, we find that when put on a purely voluntary basis there is a general disposition to co-operate. Without, of course, any repercussion when strictly divisional requirements are enforced. Likewise, it was learned early in our existence that this operetta *H.M.S. Pinafore* is still a popular rendition for school and church societies and it became necessary to politely decline to loan any uniform, or part thereof, for any purpose whatsoever.

Swimming classes are formed at periodic intervals and non-swimmers enrolled. Arrangements are effected with the local Y.M.C.A. so that division members are included in the regular evening class which is a part of that activity's curriculum.

A division fund is maintained by the supply officer under the supervision of a committee of enlisted men selected by enlisted men. Assessments are only called for as required and are usually limited to one-half a drill pay which, when levied, includes all organized officers and men. We have adhered strictly to one principle in connection with our entire existence—we will not solicit outside monetary or material aid from the community. We do not sponsor dances or lotteries and in contradistinction to many organizations, remain a completely self-sufficient group. Rather do we take pride in enlightening the public with the fact we are an economic asset and offer as proof the pay roll, rentals, and purchases resulting from our franchise.

In general, the motive behind all outside activities is to engender an increased interest in the organization and to support a justifiable pride of membership. Every effort is made to reduce the emphasis on the remunerative feature of association and to sell the idea of a unique, instructive, healthful avocation fostering as its ideal better citizenship. It must be remembered that while disciplinary measures are available theoretically, in actual practice the only instrument of discipline is transfer from active membership. Thus every element of the system of administration is predicated on the willing co-operation of the individual to the improvement of the organization as a whole.

Earlier in this article the attribute of creative genius was referred to. Our problem of training by simulation and verbal instruction in the conversion of a son of the farm to a man-o'-war's man is equally as difficult as would be the problem of the academic transformation of a salt water habitué to an acceptable tiller of the soil. With the obvious impracticability of providing the actual implements of the naval and marine profession, we do the next best thing—we simulate these devices. In one corner of our drill floor we elevate a platform and fit it out artificially to represent a bridge. Extending out across the drill floor we paint the outline of a destroyer deck. Unfortunate that we are, we must constantly bear in mind the transposition which requires the bridge force to be facing aft. Collision drill is rendered acceptable by the manufacture of a miniature mat and its application over a classroom bench. Ingenious electrical spotting boards and the employment of a photoelectric cell on a movable target give gunnery drills a touch of realism. A submarine chaser assigned renders invaluable aid in practical application of the theory disseminated at armory drills. Again creative ingenuity provides desirable substitutes for navigational and other equipment not possible of installation on so small a vessel. One salient example of the failure of improved family relations became apparent when an irate housewife discovered the motor from her vacuum cleaner supplying the motive power for an automatic speed, breakdown and man-overboard control. This vessel affords the best possible medium for training and frequent weekend cruises, subsistence being at the individual reservist's expense, and gives splendid opportunity for indoctrination. The experience gained in operating at 12 knots in a river channel maintained at minimum depths sufficient to permit, for much of its length, a scant 2 feet under the keel and with navigational aids not too far removed from the age of "dog-bark sailors" gives a degree of self-confidence and practical experience difficult to be improved upon.

Peculiarly it is felt that while, of course, pretentious armory buildings and equipment are highly desirable, too much emphasis is placed on their actual value. Rather, it is believed, the lack is too often erroneously considered to be the obstacle to more acceptable results. Just what results could be achieved with a splendid armory to house the unit, provide every convenience for drills and training, and offer recreational facilities to the limit of imagination, with, as coast divisions are blessed, actual ships of the Navy to inspect and train on, I do not presume to depict herein has only been recited what is being done in a Corn Belt city, far removed from salt water, situated on the banks of the sluggish Illinois, and using an improvised dance hall which has had to be shared with the W.P.A. recreational units. That an acceptable job is done is attested by the fact that for years this unit has consistently been in the extreme upper bracket of reserve divisions in annual merit. The work is fun and we love it or we wouldn't be doing it. It is no one-man job nor a job which calls for but one evening each Wednesday for drills and two weeks in the summer for training duty. Officers and men alike devote innumerable hours in work for the division. Employers must be contacted to secure leaves of absence for the men to cruise. Paper work too voluminous to itemize takes hours away from business pursuits and recreational time with the family. This time can't be expressed in dollars and cents and no one wishes it to be; we just thoroughly enjoy the effort needed to permit us to continue to claim association with the Mother Service and to prepare ourselves to the limit of our ability to be able to acceptably take our place in the line, if and when the Navy needs us.

"'A Project So Unique'"

7

A. Denis Clift

U.S. Naval Institute *Proceedings*
(June 2014): 72–75

THE HEADLINE ANNOUNCED: "Edmond J. Moran is Dead at 96: Admiral Led Tug Fleet on D-Day." It marked the passing of one of the most influential figures in 20th-century U.S. shipping history.[1] The U.S. Naval Institute conducted a series of interviews with Rear Admiral Moran in 1977 and published his oral history in 2004.[2] In it, he traced his childhood in Brooklyn, New York, and his joining the Moran Towing Company in 1915 as a teenager. He worked on board the tugs during summer vacations and then launched a 69-year career that would take him from office boy, to president, to chairman of the Board of Directors. The company had been founded in 1860 by his grandfather, Michael, an Irish immigrant who had had his start in the United States driving mules on the Erie Canal.

Moran's father died at a young age, and Edmond was greatly influenced by his stepfather, Thomas Reynolds, a Moran seagoing tug master whom he crewed under and greatly admired, a man who taught him much about seamanship, navigation, and the handling of tug men, which would serve him well later in his career.

On 6 April 1917, the U.S. Congress declared war on Germany. A month later, Moran enlisted in the Naval Reserve as a quartermaster third-class. He was 5-feet-6, weighed 114 pounds and, by his account, took two tries to pass the physical exam. His first assignment was to a "break-down gang" relieving crews on merchant ships taken over by the Navy.[3]

Next, Moran received his reserve commission via 90-day officers' training school, joined the coal-burning reefer ship *Ice King,* became navigator, and headed out on transatlantic runs delivering tons of frozen meat to the troops in France. When the war ended, he returned to Moran Towing. His new Navy credentials served him well as he ascended the company ladder. The Moran tug fleet was expanding. There was good growth in the tug and towing business between East Coast ports and in the Port of New York with its 1,500 square miles of waterfront, more than 700 linear miles of docks and wharves, and nonstop arrivals, departures, and inner-harbor comings and goings of thousands of merchant ships, liners, and barges. In the late 1930s, the Department of the Navy's Bureau of Ships consulted with him on the design of a new ATF fleet ocean tug, "inquiries with respect to the hull, as to deck fittings, towing apparatus, navigational equipment, the power plant, and propulsion machinery. . . . The ships, the tugs, were built on the East Coast and on the Lakes and turned out very satisfactorily." He would also consult on the Navy's plans for the new ATR rescue tug.[4]

Small-Craft Acquisition

In spring 1941, by then in charge of the towing company, Moran again took leave and headed to Washington, D.C., at the request of retired Rear Admiral Emory S. Land, chairman of the U.S. Maritime Commission, to become a special assistant in charge of acquisitions of small craft for the Army, Navy, and the British. This was a business that would grow quickly. Requests and instructions came via the Office of the Chief of Naval Operations. He and his staff negotiated with civilian boat owners, from yachts, to tugs and barges, to 75- to 80-foot sea boats of the West

Coast sardine fleet. Where necessary, three Circuit Court of Appeals judges ruled on just compensation.

"Harold Vanderbilt had a yacht, *Bara*," Moran recalled, "and we requisitioned it. It was in an unfinished state, and we determined $300,000. So he said, 'Do you ever come to New York? I don't like to go down to Washington.'

"I said, 'Yes, I do.'

"And he said, 'Let me know when you are coming to New York; give me a ring.' So in due course, I gave him a ring, and I met him at a club over there—downtown. We sat down and he said, 'What do you think that thing is worth?'

"And I said, 'We determined $300,000.'

"And he said, 'That's all right; I'll take it.' So we finished lunch, and when he got the check [for $300,000] he signed it over to the USO. He just endorsed the check over, the whole thing, which was very fitting."[5]

In May 1942, while serving under Rear Admiral Land, Moran returned to active duty as a Naval Reserve lieutenant commander, and six months later was promoted to commander. He kept moving, always upward, next serving a brief tour on loan from the Maritime Administration. At this point in the war, German U-boats were still taking a heavy toll on allied merchant shipping. Moran became rescue officer for the Eastern Sea Frontier, in charge of the operations of rescue tugs going to the aid of torpedoed and shelled merchantmen.

A Call from Admiral King

One day in 1943, a member of Chief of Naval Operations Admiral Ernest J. King's staff called on him. "He asked me a lot about ground tackle and beach operations, but he didn't tell me why he was asking the questions. He asked me about unloading on beaches. He was a naval officer, and I told him all I could."

In late 1943, Admiral Harold R. Stark, commander, U.S. Naval Forces Europe, got in touch with him. "He said, 'I might like to have you come over and take a look at a plan that is being considered. You come to London and spend a few days. Give me your opinion of certain aspects of it and go home. . . .' The next thing I knew, the Army called and asked for a type of unit that could get up on the beach and be discharged when the tide was low."[6] The Army and the Navy did not then have the craft required.

At the outset, while Moran did not know that the precise challenge would be to put 10,000 tons of gasoline, ammunition, and K-ration meals on the beaches of Normandy, he thought through the problem with some of his seafaring colleagues. They first thought that railroad-car floats—very long at 220 feet with very low 7- to 8-foot sides—might do the job. They could go up on the beach and when the tide dropped the barges would be high, dry, and ready for off-loading. But the railroad barges' lack of longitudinal strength was a worry. They wondered if oil barges might be better. "They were flat, they were a little deeper, and they had better sides so that they were more immune to the dangers of breaking in half on the way over to France."

They hedged their bets and requisitioned both railroad-car floats and oil barges. To solve the longitudinal-weakness problem, they stacked two floats on top of another in drydock and welded them together. Each had the capacity to lift 1,000 tons. A convoy of stacked floats and eight oil barges towed by tugs steaming at six knots departed the United States in late April and crossed the Atlantic with the loss of a single tug. "We took them to Cardiff, where the barges were dismantled and put afloat on their own bottoms and brought to Plymouth, where they were loaded with ammunition, K rations, and gasoline. . . . On June 6 we took them across the Channel, and they were a lifesaver."[7]

Moran was already in England in April when the barge and float convoy arrived. He had signed secrecy agreements, and in meetings with new U.S. and British colleagues he was working his way into what would be his next, far-greater assignment. General Dwight D. Eisenhower, Supreme Allied Commander of the Allied Expeditionary Force, had been studying the issue for many months. He had a clear appreciation of the near-countless challenges he would face in the D-Day landings. The beaches of Normandy had been chosen in the greatest secrecy, with the knowledge that the Germans would expect the landings to be at the ports of Cherbourg or Calais. At the same time, he would write: "The history or centuries clearly shows that the English Channel is subject to destructive storms at all times of the year. . . . The only certain method to assure supply and maintenance was by capture of large port facilities. . . . To solve this apparently unsolvable problem we undertook a project so unique as to be classed by scoffers as completely fantastic. It was a plan to construct artificial harbors on the coast of Normandy."[8]

"Two Large Synthetic Harbors"

In his 7 June communication to Soviet Marshal Josef Stalin on the Allied landings, British Prime Minister Winston Churchill wrote: "Most especially secret. We are planning to construct very quickly two large synthetic harbors on the beaches of this wide sandy bay of the Seine estuary. Great ocean liners will be able to discharge and run by numerous piers supplies to the fighting troops. This must be quite unexpected by the enemy, and will enable the buildup to proceed with very great independence of weather conditions."[9]

The artificial harbors would consist of Gooseberries—outer lines of ships scuttled bow to stern to form breakwaters—and 146 Mulberries—inner, fixed breakwaters, each displacing from 1,600 tons to 7,000 tons and made of giant concrete caissons ranging up to 5 stories high, 200 feet long, 69 feet in beam, and with a draft of 23 feet. More than 330,000 cubic yards of concrete and 31,000 tons of steel were involved in their construction, and thousands of workers were brought in for the job.

As every British shipyard building way and drydock was already fully occupied, the Allies improvised. Close to the banks of the Thames River, excavators dug 12 large holes. With pumps draining water that was seeping in, the Mulberries were constructed in the holes. When they were at a point were they could be floated, the strip of land between them and the river was removed, and they were launched.

There would be two Mulberry artificial harbors, one for the British landing at Gold Beach and one for the Americans at Omaha Beach. The British naval planning staff had to arrange, taking into account precise water depths, for the sinking of the right caissons in the correct offshore positions. The Mulberries when submerged and connected provided piers for troop and cargo ships and had more than seven miles of attached, flexible, floating roadways and pontoon bridges leading straight to the shore.[10]

Moran thought the idea of creating Mulberry harbors was reasonable. But he had been going aboard U.S. and Allied tugs and was concerned that some of the planning for the tug men might not yet be adequate to allow correct delivery of the inshore caissons. Although he was carrying out several other assignments for Admiral Stark at the time, he discussed the problem with the British officer in charge of the towing operation, who went to his superiors and said, "This guy can do this job better than I can do it. Let me out and put him in." The issue was taken to Royal Navy Admiral Sir Bertram Ramsey, Operation Neptune Naval Commander-in-Chief of the Allied Naval Expeditionary Force. After Ramsey and Stark conferred, Ramsey told Moran that he was to relieve the Royal Navy captain who had been charged with being the controller of the operation.[11] Naval Reserve Captain Edmond J. Moran was now in charge of the tugboat fleet, 150–160 strong.

Moran kept circulating among the tug crews on the British coast, refining plans, moving equipment, keeping morale high; "they never knew when we might get an air raid or we'd get one of these buzz bombs." He selected a Dutch tug as the lead boat for the cross-channel operation, thinking a crew whose country had been overrun would have the right esprit for the return to the continent. "The next fellow I sent was an American. . . . I just talked to him; he [later became] president of one of our companies in Baltimore. He was a game sort of guy."[12]

"90 Caissons in Tow"

The D-Day assault took place early morning on 6 June. Moran had 90 caissons to tow. He recalled in his oral history: "We started across with the tows on the morning of June 6. The tows proceeded at a rate of five to six knots, and the distance was approximately 100 miles, coming from Portsmouth, Selsey, and Plymouth." All of the tug crews "were civilians, and they were capable of doing it all right. And, of course, there were patrols there that would lead them in, because they were under constant fire from the shore batteries. . . . [I]t all worked according to plan; we brought the equipment over, all of it, and the British engineers and the American engineers had the job of locating them where they wanted them.[13]

Mulberry A at Omaha was in operation on 16 June. The contrast between Omaha on 6 June and 12 days later, in Samuel Eliot Morison's words, was amazing:

This lonely three-mile stretch of beach, where nothing bigger than a small fishing boat had ever landed, was now a major port of entry. Through 18 June it had received 197,444 troops, 27,340 vehicles, and 68,799 long tons of supplies. With the aid of Mulberry A, Omaha had now become the most active port in northern France, with the greatest capacity. And, for the moment, it was the most active port in Europe, with British Beach Gold a good second.[14]

While Mulberry A would be severely, irreparably damaged in a violent storm in late June, it had played its part in establishing the Normandy beachhead and facilitating the initial U.S. moves inland. Mulberry B would continue in a major artificial-harbor role for months. "I don't think the assault on France could have been accomplished with out it," Admiral Moran reflected:

I don't think there was a possibility of going on open beaches without the protection that these harbors afforded. I don't think it could have been completed in half the time that it took for the whole adventure to be completed if you hadn't done it that way. It would have taken twice as long. These troops were going ashore over the caissons, over the road. In seven days, the bridge had been completed. The LST could have gotten them up onto the beach, but the LST would have been shot to pieces, and the crews did very well getting them over the pontoon bridges. They had lots of artillery, and they didn't have to worry about stepping into water over their heads. We landed them and got them on the bridge, and they walked ashore and went where they were supposed to go and got there safely.[15]

Breakfast with Ike

In mid-June, Moran, now back in London, was ordered to report to the destroyer USS *Thompson* (DD-627) in Portsmouth, and as it was 0500, he went down to the wardroom for breakfast. "Pretty soon a fellow came along, sitting alongside me . . . and it was Eisenhower. So I said, 'Good morning, General.' He said 'Can I get some breakfast here?' I said 'Sure, just a minute. Mine's coming.'" The *Thompson* had been providing gunfire support during the landings and on the 12th had carried General Eisenhower, General George C. Marshall, Admiral King, and General Henry H. Arnold to take a look at the invasion beaches. After some food, Eisenhower pulled Moran aside on the destroyer, told him how desperate he was for more supplies and equipment from the United States to keep the invasion going, and ordered him back to the United States—nothing in writing—to carry that message to all the right people and right places. "Then I saw Marshall and King," Moran recalled. "King said to me, 'I saw that place you built there at Normandy, and I must say it was a great job.'"[16]

While Moran personally downplayed his D-Day role, he was awarded the Legion of Merit; the Honorary Commander, Military Division, Order of the British Empire; and the French Croix de Guerre with gold stars. He departed for Guam and when the war ended was guiding the preparation of Mulberries for the invasion of Japan. In 1953, he was promoted to Naval Reserve rear admiral. He returned to Moran Towing, was elected chairman of the Board of Directors in 1964, and retired in 1984.[17]

Notes

1. The *New York Times*, 17 July 1993.
2. *The Reminiscences of Rear Admiral Edmond J. Moran, U.S. Naval Reserve (Retired)*, Interviewed by Dr. John T. Mason Jr. (Annapolis, MD: U.S. Naval Institute, 2004).
3. Ibid., 15
4. Ibid., 32–33.
5. Ibid., 50–51.
6. Ibid., 62.
7. Ibid., 64–66.
8. Dwight D. Eisenhower, *Crusade in Europe* (Garden City, NY: Doubleday & Company, Inc. 1948), 234.
9. Winston S. Churchill, *Triumph and Tragedy* (Boston: Houghton Mifflin Company, 1953), 8.
10. CDR Kenneth Edwards, RN, *Operation Neptune* (London:The Albatross Library, 1947), 60–63.
11. Moran, op. cit., 71.
12. Ibid., 78
13. Ibid., 72–75.
14. Samuel Eliot Morison, *History of United States Naval Operations in World War II*, vol. 11, *The Invasion of France and Germany 1944–1945*, (Boston: Little, Brown, 1953; Naval Institute Press Edition, 2011), 166.
15. Moran, op. cit., 76.
16. Ibid., 84–85.
17. *Tow Line* magazine, vol. 46 (Winter 1993–94), 5.

Mr. Clift is the U.S. Naval Institute's vice president for planning and operations and president emeritus of the National Intelligence University. A naval officer from 1958–62, he served in the administrations of 11 successive U.S. Presidents. From 1963–66, he was editor-in-chief of *Proceedings*.

8 "World War II Subchasers"

Theodore R. Treadwell

(Selections from chapters 2, 3, and 4 of *Splinter Fleet:
The Wooden Subchasers of World War II*,
Naval Institute Press, 2000): 16–46.

World War II Subchasers

The ascendancy of Adolf Hitler, threatening the involvement of the
United States in a second world war, revived urgent interest in an antisubmarine shipbuilding program. By 1938 history began repeating itself
with astonishing similarity to the events of 1916. Germany was at war
with Britain and France, and their U-boats were again roaming the seas
at will, sinking tens of thousands of tons of Allied shipping. Franklin D.
Roosevelt, now president, called for an all-out construction program for
subchasers as a stopgap. There being only one antisubmarine vessel on
the entire East Coast (USCG cutter *Dione*), the navy again had to make
do with hastily recruited YPs, minesweepers, motor launches, sailing
vessels, and a "hooligan navy" of privately owned yachts and trawlers.
Alfred Loring Swasey, by then semiretired, was commissioned to come
up with a suitable design for a new subchaser, once again to be made of
wood, since steel as in the earlier war was reserved for bigger ships. The
hull length of 110 feet and the use of some fifty small boatyards around
the country matched the subchaser building program of the earlier war.

In 1939 a competition for a suitable subchaser design was arranged between Luders Marine Construction Company of Stamford, Connecticut, an experienced World War I boatbuilder, and Electric Boat Company (Elco) of Bayonne, New Jersey, maker of PT boats. This led to an experimental subchaser built from each design, the SC 449 and SC 450. Of these, the Luders SC 449 became the design of choice. Launched in May 1940, she was commissioned that September, the prototype of all 438 SC subchasers built during the war. The SC 449 played an unspectacular role as a training ship during much of the war until January 1945, when she became the guinea pig for a top secret experiment.

A third design, SC 453, was powered by two new "pancake" type diesel engines, capable of driving the ships at speeds up to 21 knots. The pancake equipped SC became the prototype for the World War II wooden subchaser, but only 243 SCs received pancake engines. The remaining 195 were powered by General Motors straight-S diesels (8-268A 500 hp). Although these had top speeds of only fifteen knots, they performed the same duties as the pancake-equipped SCs. The SCs with pancake engines had variable-pitch propellers and were easier to maneuver than those with the 286A diesels. In addition, the pancake engines were lighter in weight, reducing the stern draft by eighteen inches. The reason all subchasers were not equipped with pancake engines and variable pitch propellers was a matter of urgency. Production of pancake engines could not meet demand at a time when vessels to fight the U-boat war were a critical need.

One might inquire why the size and general configuration of the second generation SCs were so similar to those of their antecedents. At first glance the newly designed SCs looked hardly different from those of World War I. Both hulls were 110 feet long, and each had a distinctive rub rail running two-thirds the length of the vessel, three feet above the waterline. Both had guns mounted forward and aft, with a stubby little pilothouse amidships. The flared "whaleboat" bow and a low silhouette were common to both. But the second-generation design, officially designated the SC-497 class, was two feet wider at the beam than the SC-I class. Another major difference was the means of propulsion, the earlier version being triple-screwed with gasoline engines and the newer version twin screwed with diesel engines. The pilothouses on the new chasers were made of cast aluminum instead of wood. The newer ones were equipped with sophisticated sonar gear, rocket depth-charge launchers (mousetraps), and 3-inch/50 or 40-mm guns forward instead of the old 3-inch/23 cannons. Most were equipped with radar, although many of them were not so equipped until the war was almost over. The major differences between the two generations of subchasers was not so much in the hulls as it was in the greater sophistication of electronic gear on the later vessels.

To a yachtsman's eye, the lines of a subchaser's hull were rather pleasing, with a graceful flare at the bow and a fluid fore-to-aft sweep worthy of admiration—were it not for the homely, tugboat like pilothouse jutting up amidships and a deck hopelessly cluttered with guns, ordnance, and other gear.

The nomenclature for SCs has been confusing. In World War I the SCs were identified by the letters "PC" followed by a number. "PC 225" was, for example, actually SC 225. At the start of World War II the same numbering series was continued, with the result that the first vessels built were initially listed as PCs. Then in October 1942 the nomenclature was changed to "SC" to differentiate the 110-foot wooden-hulled subchasers from the larger 173-foot steel-hulled patrol craft, which were more accurately designated "PC." But many SCs slid down the ways after that with the letters "PC," later to be changed by the crews to SC.

World War II the SC-497 class had a normal complement of three officers and twenty-four enlisted men, a cruising radius of fifteen hundred miles, and speeds from fifteen to twenty-one knots, depending upon the type of drive. Typical SC armament consisted of eight rocket-propelled "mousetrap" depth charges mounted on the bow, a 40-mm or 3-inch/50 cannon forward of the pilothouse, three 20-mm Oerlikon antiaircraft guns aft, and fourteen or more 300-pound depth charges on racks or rails and K-guns toward the stern. Many SCs mounted an additional .50-caliber machine gun on the flying bridge or at the fantail. An assortment of small arms, including Thompson submachine guns, completed the arsenal.

Although the United States was not officially at war until 7 December 1941, keels for eighty-four SCs had already been laid before that date. The average construction time from keel-laying to launching was six months, but many were built in less time. Elizabeth City Shipyard, Elizabeth City, North Carolina, set a record when on 6 April 1942 it launched SC 704 only thirty days after laying the keel.[1] Most of the forty-nine boatyards where they were built were small, family-owned enterprises employing highly skilled craftsmen, some of them having built SCs during World War I. Details for quality construction were meticulously spelled out in quaint, wooden-boat terms reminiscent of nineteenth-century whaling or clipper ships. The hull planking must be long-leaf yellow pine. Planking butts shall be carefully laid out so as to have as wide a distribution as practicable and so as not to conflict with butts or scarphs of planksheer, clamps, shelf and other longitudinals. Planking to be caulked with oakum and cotton, sprayed with paint, and filled with putty. The decking to be of Douglas fir or white pine edge grain, the mast of Sitka spruce, hollow, built up construction. The stem to be of white oak, side 7 [inches], built up and molded with deadwood apron and knee. A mahogany steering wheel with four complete turns of wheel to throw rudder head to port or starboard. The hawse pipe to be of trumpet type, fitted at stem head to form a fair mooring eye.[3]

The boatyards adhered as closely as they could to specifications but often used woods or materials most readily available in their individual areas. As it turned out, it didn't matter; there wasn't a "lemon" in the entire subchaser fleet. Thanks to the craftsmen who put them together, every one of the 438 subchasers built for World War II proved to be strong, tough, sturdy, seaworthy vessels, as any man who ever sailed on one will tell you.

That they were seaworthy, buoyant, and safe in almost any sea, however, offered little comfort to the sailors who for months on end endured cramped quarters, poor ventilation, damp or moldy bedding, water shortage, and the incessant—often violent—pitching and rolling. If the bedding wasn't wet, it was damp. If it wasn't damp, it was moldy. There was never enough time or sunshine when in port to air bedding thoroughly, particularly in the Atlantic and other waters in the Northern Hemisphere. Noxious diesel fumes from exhausts on each side of the hull at the waterline bathed the ship in a sharp, sickening, odoriferous aura, recalled with extreme distaste by all SC veterans.

. . . The forward compartment, a space about eighteen feet long by ten feet wide, was the living quarters for sixteen men. The men slept in tiered pipe bunks that were folded against the bulkhead when not in use. Men who wanted to sleep had to put up with others in the lighted compartment who were playing cards, talking, or as was often the case, arguing. Eight men occupied the after crew's quarters, sharing their space with the ship's company during mess, which was prepared three times daily (when the cook wasn't seasick) in the cramped galley. In addition to his folding pipe berth, each man had a shelf and a small locker for all of his gear and personal possessions. His private world was not much bigger than a refrigerator.

No one knows for sure which generation of sailors suffered the rougher ride, since both were uncomfortable even in moderate seas. The heavy roll combined with a violent pitching motion, resulting in a harsh, incessant, corkscrew pounding that permitted neither sleep nor rest for anyone. In both wars creature comforts on the subchasers consisted of cramped, often damp or downright wet quarters, no bathing or washing facilities, and long periods when there was a scarcity of fresh water and palatable food. Meals at sea were plain, scanty, and cold, since ship's cooks, as a group, were notoriously prone to seasickness. On rough trips it was almost every man for himself.

In the early days of the war the sole purpose of the SCs was to hamper, deter, and slow down the U-boat offensive in order to give the United States time to build destroyers, destroyer escorts, and antisubmarine aircraft to wage all-out war against the U-boats. The wooden subchasers and their larger sister ships, the 173-foot steel-hulled PCs, were intended to serve more as stopgaps than as offensive weapons. Armed with depth charges, the SCs and PCs screened merchant convoys with their underwater sound gear, keeping the U-boats submerged and on the defensive, unable to launch their torpedoes.

While most SCs at some time during the war were equipped with radar, a few had none until the war was almost over, making necessary the constant use of a lookout in the crow's nest while under way. . . .

The deck of an SC was as crowded as the compartments below. The only open space was the quarterdeck immediately aft of the pilothouse, a space approximately eight by seven feet surrounded by a disarray of flag bag, ready lockers, ventilators, Charley Noble (galley stack), antiaircraft guns, and the engine room hatch. One had to be nimble to avoid obstructions while making his way about the ship, whether topside or below decks. It helped to be of medium or small build. Jim Moyer, a big, burly sonarman on the 648, was forever banging some part of his body into a projection or sharp object, resulting in an eruption like "Ow! This goddamned ship was built for midgets!" and sending his shipmates into convulsions.

The speedy construction and deployment of SCs in 1942 was a good beginning, but everyone knew that the little ships were no match for the U-boats, especially if they ran into one on the surface. Still, they were a big improvement over fishing trawlers and private motor yachts because of their greater maneuverability, longer cruising radius, and heavier armament. A surfaced sub could outshoot, outrun, and outmaneuver a subchaser, but no U-boat commander would be foolish enough to surface in the presence of a subchaser unless he was certain no other ships were nearby, which was rarely the case. By keeping submarines submerged and thereby unable to take periscope aim, SCs proved to be an effective deterrent. A submerged U-boat was forced to operate solely on batteries, draining its only source of power. The SC could track with its sonar and make repeated depth-charge attacks while notifying other ships and radioing for backup.

Of course, in the unlikely event it surfaced, the submarine could retire to a comfortable distance and take its time shooting the subchaser out of the water. The navy's standing rule was that the SC was to ram at flank speed any surfaced enemy submarine it might encounter, a rule fraught with high risk and considerable danger—most likely death— to the subchaser. A ninety-five-ton wooden ship ramming a steel-plated submarine, ten times heavier and fully armed, would be like crashing full speed into an immovable steel jetty on which men were shooting at you point blank with cannon and machine guns. The 4-inch deck guns on the U-boats had considerably more power and range than either the 3-inch/50 or the 40-mm guns of the SC. Every man who served on a subchaser knew these facts, and while he assumed a "come what may" attitude, he felt much more comfortable when his ship was escorting a convoy in company with other escorts.

SCs continued convoy and patrol work throughout the war, even when larger destroyer escorts and destroyers became available in quantity. The Battle of the Atlantic did not begin to change in our favor until the spring of 1943, when destroyer escorts and destroyers teamed with vigilant and aggressive air patrols to form killer groups that methodically searched for and destroyed the U-boats. As deterrents, SCs more than proved their value. But unlike the SCs of World War I, which were used solely for antisubmarine patrol, the new generation of SCs would be used for many other purposes suitable for their size and capabilities. As control vessels in amphibious landings, shallow water minesweepers, smoke layers, air-sea rescue ships, ferryboats, antisub patrol and other missions, the SCs were invaluable.

From landings in the Mediterranean at Palermo, Salerno, Anzio, and Southern France, they proved themselves gutsy and indispensable. At Normandy they were invaluable. In the Pacific they were used as control boats in assaults at Lae, Finschhafen, Hollandia, Cape Gloucester, Leyte, Guam, Saipan, Kwajalein, Eniwetok, Iwo Jima, Okinawa, and countless other bloody beaches. Their shallow draft and maneuverability gave rise to the conversion during the war of seventy SCs to SCCs-subchaser control vessels.[4] The conversion provided additional radio equipment and sleeping quarters for extra radio and radar personnel who came aboard during amphibious operations. These communication teams not only directed the assault waves on D-Day but remained aboard, sometimes for as long as two weeks after the invasion, to serve as a communications and traffic-control center between beach and landing boats.[5]

One veteran SC sailor wrote recently: "We went to sea on a wooden ship as the smallest combatant ship in the U.S. Navy. We went everywhere the big ships went and to many places the big ships were unable to go . . . [t]hose of us who served . . . knew we had truly gone to sea and performed our duty."[6]

The tales that can be told about the SCs are like those of Mr. Roberts and McHale's Navy, and they are legion. That subchasers and their men were not exactly "regular Navy" was all too true, yet they managed to prevail, riding out the war in grubby splendor and humble fortitude.

Subchaser Training Center

As the United States entered World War II, concurrently with the program of construction of subchasers, the navy faced the huge task of recruiting and training men to operate them. Few people today realize the magnitude of the job they faced, or how much they accomplished in those first few desperate months after Pearl Harbor. Caught completely by surprise, the navy sprang into action immediately by recalling warrant and chief petty officers who had recently retired. Many of them did not have to be recalled. They reenlisted the day after Pearl Harbor. They were the specialists the chief boatswain's mates, signalmen, machinist's mates yeomen, gunner's mates whose lifetime careers had been devoted to the navy. They were the ones who could give hands-on training to the green landlubbers enlisting in droves all over the country.

In addition, instructors and professors from leading colleges and universities were offered commissions in the Naval Reserve. They knew nothing about the navy, ships, or the sea, and they admitted it. But once they were given the rudiments of codes, communications, diesel engines, operation of sonar gear, radar, navigation, damage control, antisubmarine tactics, aircraft recognition, electricity the subject didn't really matter they knew how to make up a teaching manual and teach from the book. I have had much schooling during my life, but some of my finest instructors were men in the navy who admitted they didn't really know the subject but merely knew how to teach it.

Subchasers needed officers as well as enlisted men. The navy offered commissions to students in their final year at college and graduate schools with active duty deferred until June 1942 to allow them to get their degrees before donning their uniforms. It was a smart tactic, enabling the navy to get a jump on local draft boards, some of whom were selecting draftees strictly by lottery, a flawed system whereby a potential Ph.D., M.D., or electrical engineer could wind up in the army as a buck private. The recruitment strategy paid off. All across the country, thousands of fourth year and graduate students at colleges and universities eagerly signed up to become commissioned officers in the United States Naval Reserve, ready to report for active duty upon completion of their studies that June. Most of these were sent to officer training schools for ninety days of rigorous physical and classroom training, emerging at the end of this period as "ninety-day wonders."

In March 1942, Cdr. Eugene F. McDaniel, a thirty-eight-year-old Annapolis graduate, was given the job of setting up and running a naval training center in Miami called SCTC, the Subchaser Training Center. McDaniel, a thin, lanky, bespectacled Virginian who looked more like a college professor than a sailor experienced in submarine warfare, was a man of decisive action, a doer. He had a fiery, fanatical hatred for the enemy, particularly all Nazis. Having served thirteen years on destroyers in the Atlantic, he never forgot the time when, before the United States was officially in the war, his ship had answered an SOS to pick up seamen off a torpedoed British ship. He found their lifeboats, all eight unarmed, riddled by machine-gun slugs, and full of blood and bodies.

The first thing he did when he got to Miami was to get a lifeboat, spatter it with about forty bullet holes, splash realistically painted blood stains around its insides, and set it up as "Exhibit A" outside the entrance to the training center. Every Monday he would personally address each incoming class, using the lifeboat as illustration. He began by telling the men that there was no time to consider their individual desires. They were there to learn a tough job, and quickly. Each man in all likelihood would face a situation where he alone would be responsible for ten Allied ships and their crews. The speech would wind down with a blistering diatribe of hatred for the Nazis and the Japanese. Pointing to the lifeboat he would exhort, "See what they do? Deliberately and callously machine-gun defenseless sailors as they float in their lifeboat. The Nazis are nothing but inhumane, ruthless murderers, and you and I will put a stop to it." His fiery denunciation was something no one who heard it would ever forget.

When McDaniel arrived on the scene in March 1942, SCTC occupied the old Clyde Mallory pier, commonly known as Pier Two. The building, which overlooked Biscayne Bay, was noisy and poorly ventilated, and the classrooms, separated by thin partitions, were hardly ideal. He had only four officers to help him. They had to find places for the first class of twenty students to eat, sleep, and study. The staff worked around the clock outlining courses, arranging classes, deciding on curriculum, and teaching, some of which McDaniel did himself.

Their objective was clearly defined: The subchasers and PCs, and later the destroyer escorts more than fifteen hundred ships had to be manned with men and officers properly trained to perform their duties of escort and patrol. The pressure was intense; submarines were roaming the East Coast at will, sinking ships in alarming numbers. Subchasers under highest priority were coming off the ways from scores of shipyards. Crews had to be trained and ready as fast as the ships were launched.

The navy had picked the right man, for McDaniel knew how to reduce red tape to a minimum. When channels of communication with Washington were too slow, he acted upon his own, at times stepping on toes but getting the job accomplished. He was helped by the tremendous sense of urgency everyone felt.

After SCTC hit its stride, a typical week for officers would be as follows:

Monday: Four hours of classroom instruction in antisubmarine warfare (ASW), one hour for lunch, one hour of medical instruction (on many SCs the captain was the ship's doctor unless a pharmacist's mate formed part of the roster), three more hours on ASW.

Tuesday: Two hours of medical instruction, two hours of sonar and ASW, followed by an exam. In the afternoon, out to sea on an SC or a YP for seamanship drills.

Wednesday: Two hours' instruction in communications; one hour of sonar and ASW; medical exam; four hours of sonar and ASW in afternoon.

Thursday: Docking practice aboard an SC; ASW and radar instruction.

Friday: Five hours of ASW; radar exam; two hours of navigation instruction.

Saturday: All day at sea with drills in gunnery, communications, ship handling, and "tentative command."

An entire week at SCTC was spent on instruction in various types of ordnance, including mousetraps, depth charges, ammunition, pyrotechnics, fire control doctrine, etc. Loading drills were conducted on 40-mm, 3-inch/50, and 20-mm guns and .50-caliber machine guns; battery control drills and small arms instruction were included, all thoroughly interspersed with exams. The only time off for officers-in-training was on alternate Sunday afternoons.

Toward the end of their six-week course, the trainees were given a three-to-five-day cruise to familiarize them with an understanding of enlisted functions while under way. Student officers stood deck watches, manned the helm, trained the guns, operated sound gear, and saw duty as quartermaster and in the engine room. Each student was instructed to bring aboard "1 small hand bag, 2 bath towels, 1 set shaving gear, 1 soap, 1 comb, 3 khaki uniforms (wear one) without coat, 1 skivvies, 2 handkerchiefs, 2 sox, 1 toothbrush and powder, 1 notebook and pencil."[1]

Thanks to Commander McDaniel, in its four years of existence SCTC became a legendary model as a training center. The reserve officers who survived the rigorous six weeks of intensive training would never forget it. The Miami facility set standards that were followed by dozens of naval training centers all over the country. The SCTC type of operational training, developed and proven effective for ASW vessels, proved to be valuable for other ships. Some officers trained at SCTC were assigned to other classes of ships like destroyer escorts (DEs) and destroyers (DDs). By 1945 SCTC had become Miami's biggest business, overflowing into ten hotels on Biscayne Boulevard and extending into a dozen piers on the waterfront.

Over twenty-five thousand officers and fifty-seven thousand enlisted men were trained at SCTC, including officers from Russia, Brazil, Cuba, and France. A total of 598 U.S. Navy ships and 79 foreign ships were shaken down by this activity.

No one knows exactly how the term "Donald Duck Navy" originated, but at some time during its existence SCTC used memo pads printed with an unofficial logo depicting an imitation Donald Duck sporting a Y-gun and depth charges. To this day old SC and PC salts talk about having been members of the Donald Duck Navy, some with pride, others grudgingly. On one point they all agree. If the Donald Duck Navy had an "Annapolis," it was SCTC, and its commandant was Cdr. Eugene F. McDaniel.

The Battle of the Atlantic

When war was declared in December of 1941 at least five German U-boats were operating freely off the east coast of the United States— coast, for all practical purposes, undefended. Adm. Adolphus Andrews, Commander, Eastern Sea Frontier, had at his disposal four yard patrol boats (YPs), four subchasers, one Coast Guard cutter, three World War I "Eagle" boats, and 103 aircraft, only five of which were combat ready. This tiny force was to protect a 28,000-square-mile area extending from the St. Lawrence River down to North Carolina. Defense forces in the Gulf of Mexico and the Caribbean were in no better shape.

The U-boats found our merchant fleet sailing unescorted and with their lights on at night. There was no radio discipline; shore stations operated as if in peacetime, broadcasting time signals and weather reports. Shoreside cities blazed with lights at night. The U-boats, hardly believing the bonanza offered them, roamed up and down the coast with impunity, sinking everything in sight. Within a period of ten days, they sank twenty-five ships totaling 200,000 tons. Not one U-boat was damaged, much less sunk.

It became a time of feverish activity for the navy, having suddenly found itself in a shooting war on two fronts, with Japan in the Pacific and Germany in the Atlantic. Keels for new second-generation SCs were just being laid. . . .

It wasn't until late in 1942 that SCs finally began coming off the ways and were quickly being commissioned for escort and patrol duty, working out of several bases along the East Coast. It was a time of testing and training for green officers and crews of the Splinter Fleet, unaccustomed to the navy and the seafaring life. It was a time in which an incorrect appraisal of a situation, a missing link in communication, an abuse of authority, or just plain inexperience could lead to an abrupt perception of reality. Getting used to the ways of the regular navy was part of every reservist's education, and often his only teacher was experience itself. New officers quickly learned the hard facts of life. Jules J. Jordy, Lt.(jg) USNR, in command of SC 638 based in Norfolk, ordered sonar from Philadelphia, something his ship badly needed for locating, tracking down, and destroying U-boats. Two weeks later, still with no sonar, after spending the morning in a fruitless search for the gear around the base, he returned to his ship and was intercepted by the quartermaster, who informed him that he was wanted in Operations immediately. Jordy knew there was a convoy forming up for a trip to Charleston and that they needed an escort, but there was no way the SC 638 could be a proper escort without sonar. A good officer and a man of decision, he marched over to Operations to tell the captain in charge that he couldn't go.

The captain was waiting for him. "Jordy, here's your TF plan, departure is set at 1500. You ready?"

"Sir, we don't have sonar gear and I don't expect it for another week or so."

The captain looked at him. "Do the Germans know that you don't have sonar?"

"No, sir."

"Then what in hell are you waiting for? Get out there and escort those ships down to Charleston."

He did.

The experience of obeying orders, no matter what, came as a severe shock to some civilians who had become officers. A day or so after newly commissioned Ens. Jonas M. Berkey reported aboard SC 1039 as third officer, the ship was ordered out into the Caribbean on patrol. As soon as it left the breakwater and entered the rough sea, Berkey, on the flying bridge, became seasick. In order to give his new officer some navigating experience, the captain told Berkey to go below to figure their position. Berkey, forgetting that he was no longer a civilian, answered he could not do that because he was sick. The captain's reaction was an immediate and blistering lecture, both personal and specific, including the threat of a court-martial unless Berkey obeyed orders. In less than a minute, the pain of seasickness was nothing compared to Berkey's fear of the captain and a court-martial. He went dutifully below to the chart room and figured their position, after which he stood a four-hour watch in constant agony from seasickness. His temporary feeling of hatred for the captain gave way to profound respect in the days to follow, for he had suddenly learned the meaning of military obedience and the strength of authority-albeit the hard way. Having been forced to work successfully even though in pain gave him a new self-confidence. Later, when he became captain of the ship, he used the same method to impress the meaning of military obedience to his men.

"Those were tough days," writes Daniel V. James, former commanding officer of SC 1 002:

Wooden ships that small were never intended to be on the high seas for extended periods making like make-believe warships. Having a signalman who didn't know code was not much different than having a C.O. with a similar level of competence and experience. We were anything but an all-star team. Rather, the Navy considered us losers to begin with—but better than nothing. We gave as good as we got. But what a way to grow up! We were close to the unforgiving sea, and took every wave in style, wet bunks and all. We learned to cope not only with the elements but with ourselves as well.

The rough and sometimes grisly work of searching for and rescuing survivors of torpedoed or mined ships or collisions was unrelenting. In the bitter cold of early morning on 7 January 1943, all standby SCs stationed at Cape May, New Jersey, were ordered out to search for survivors of an escort vessel that had been run down by a merchant ship the night before. After a few hours' search, SC 1354 found seventeen men floating in the freezing water, all wearing their lifejackets, but none alive.

A couple of weeks later SC 1354 was assigned to escort a U.S. submarine from Delaware Bay to New York Harbor a routine business if all submarines had not been vulnerable to attack from trigger-happy U.S. merchant ships, ever on the alert for U-boats. Too, SCs looked like submarines in certain seas, and here was a real submarine being escorted by a ship that looked like a submarine. Both vessels flew the biggest American flag they could find, and SC 1354 manned her signal lamp continuously, placing herself between the submarine and any ships spotted and signaling furiously to advise the other ship that they were friendly. Even so, one merchant ship they passed was at general quarters with guns trained on them and alarmingly failed to respond to the signaling; fortunately, though, the merchantman held its fire.

Beginning in May and June 1942, the Caribbean was being overrun by German U-boats. It began when six U-boats entered the Caribbean through the Florida Straits, and the Windward and Mona passages, after successfully operating in more northern waters between New York and Cape Hatteras. In May the first of four SC subchasers arrived at San Juan, Puerto Rico. SC 1279 and her men were greeted as "saviors" of Puerto Rico by the citizens of San Juan, who did not know that the 1279's sonar was inoperative because of missing parts, aside from her having no radar.

These deficiencies were corrected within a couple of weeks, and an opportunity to test their effectiveness suddenly appeared when they were escorting a merchant ship to Guantanamo Bay, Cuba. Without warning, there was a sudden explosion on the cargo vessel, and within a matter of minutes she sank. Simultaneously, the 1279 picked up a strong submarine contact and made a depth-charge attack, dropping seven charges. They waited for the seven underwater explosions, but heard only two. Five depth charges had failed to roll off, inexcusably rusted and "frozen" to the racks—due to the failure of the gunner's mates to pay more attention to maintenance. Everyone aboard the sunken merchant ship was either in a lifeboat or wearing a life jacket, and all were rescued without injury, but the incident taught SC 1279 a lesson in preparedness that her men never forgot.

The subchasers, with their green officers and crews, were pressed into duty for which they were not fully prepared, but the slaughter inflicted by U-boats was so relentless and so damaging that every means possible had to be put to use. Shakedown cruises for many subchasers were working assignments in convoy escort duty, lasting seven days or longer. The rough ocean conditions, no water-making capability, cramped and uncomfortable quarters, and poor ventilation all added up to a miserable introduction to the sea for youngsters away from home for the first time in their lives.

Still, some stories had happy endings. Ed Sullivan, on the first patrol of SC 507 out of Staten Island off the New Jersey coast, was sitting on the rail with his buddy Fogerty, who was facing outboard. They each had only two months in the navy. Sullivan suddenly noticed Fogerty's jaw drop, eyes widen. Fogerty gasped "Torpedoes!" Spinning around, Sullivan saw two wakes streaking directly at them only thirty yards away. Their hearts in their mouths, the tyros watched, transfixed, scared beyond belief. Suddenly the bubbling wakes turned 90 degrees in unison and began playing in their bow wake, dorsals curving gracefully as they broke water. Two porpoises were innocently engaged in their age-old play with a ship at sea. One didn't have to be new or green to be startled by the phosphorescent wake of porpoises at play; mariners often failed to recognize them as such at first sighting and commonly broke formation, changed courses and speeds, and tried evasive tactics until they realized their error.

Not long after this incident Sullivan, Fogerty, and the 507 found themselves engaged in the real Battle of the Atlantic. On the night of 26 February 1942, rudely awakened shortly after midnight by the sounding of general quarters, they scrambled topside for their battle stations. Less than a thousand yards on their port beam they could see a ship broken in half, engulfed in bright orange and red flames that flickered high into the night sky. In the most horrendous disaster yet to strike the American merchant fleet, the tanker *R. P. Resor* had been torpedoed by German U-boat 578. The commanding officer of the 507, Lieutenant Taylor, intensified their sonar search in an effort to make contact with the enemy sub. They spotted a life raft with three men in it. They launched the wherry, but the oil was so thick on the surface that the wherry could make no headway. Taylor had to back the 507 into the heavy oil to come alongside the raft. The survivors were so heavy with oil it took four men to drag them aboard. Two of the three men survived, out of a total of fifty men on the *R. P. Resor*. When a coast guard cutter arrived a few hours later, they transferred the survivors and the dead man and resumed their patrol. The ship burned for two days off the Jersey coast, clearly visible to crowds who thronged the seashore to watch. A few days after she sank, a story in the newspaper reported that the coast guard had been the first on the scene—incorrectly, since it was SC 507 that arrived first.

New officers frequently found themselves in situations requiring decisions for which they had no prior experience. SC 983 was in dry dock having its seams recaulked after being split open from underwater depth-charge explosions. The third officer was ordered to stay with the ship while the other two were ashore on leave. His most important duty was to sign off the daily work order as each job was completed. One day he was called to the rear of the ship where workmen were using a huge wrench and a sledgehammer to tighten the massive nuts that held the propeller shafts. The young officer had never seen the screws before—or anything else on the undersides, for that matter. The shipwrights wanted him to tell them when the nuts had been properly torqued. He looked at the foreman and said, "What do you think?" The foreman returned his look with an understanding smile and said, "I think they are pretty damn tight now." He took a deep breath, crossed his fingers, and signed.

With little experience to go on, officers in the "Donald Duck Navy" could not always count on conventional personnel assignments, either. At one time SC 998 had on its roster three chief boatswain's mates, one first-class boatswain's mate, one coxswain, and no seamen. Before this was straightened out, with little experience to go on, officers in the "Donald Duck Navy" could not always count on conventional personnel assignments, either. At one time SC 998 had on its roster three chief boatswain's mates, one first-class boatswain's mate, one coxswain, and no seamen. Before this was straightened out, no work was done except by the coxswain and the third officer. The topheaviness resulted from ship movements to three or four ports in different sea frontiers after requisitioning replacements. At each port a new chief boatswain would report aboard. Another time the same SC had three officers exactly reversed in role and rank. The commanding officer was an ensign, the executive officer was a lieutenant (jg), and the third officer was a senior grade lieutenant. Fortunately none of the officers let it bother them and the situation was eventually straightened out.

In some situations, resourcefulness had to serve where experience failed. Early in April 1942, SC 540 was placed in commission in Benton Harbor and ordered to report to New Orleans by way of the Mississippi. Having no charts, the 540 relied on road maps picked up from gas stations along the route. Along the way they tied up each night to avoid the hazards of what one man described as "logs, trees, houses and barns floating down the Big Muddy." SC 437, making the same trip some months before, put another spin on it. They tied up every night and went ashore for liberty. At every stop, crowds would gather to greet them, so rarely had anyone in those parts seen an "honest to God" warship.

No amount of experience can prepare a sailor for everything that can happen on a ship. SC 656 was in a group escorting a convoy of tankers from Galveston when she was relieved by another subchaser and ordered to proceed independently to the naval operating base (NOB) Key West. On the way the weather began to deteriorate, and the commanding officer, Lt. Edward O'Donnell, anxious to make Key West before conditions got worse, increased the ship's speed, resulting in considerable pitching and rolling. The violent motion of the ship sheered a toggle pin on one of the depth-charge racks, causing the charge to fall to the deck, where it commenced rolling from gunwale to gunwale. The crew managed to secure the charge, but it represented a serious explosion hazard if its detonator had been damaged. Determining that the safest procedure would be to drop the charge overboard, the captain had a couple of his men erect a temporary platform on the fantail so that he, the captain, could execute this maneuver. Just when everything was in position and the captain had stationed himself to shove the charge over the side, a large wave slapped him overboard. Startled, the crew sprang into action. The officer of the deck ordered all engines stopped. However, by the time life rings had been tossed, the captain was being carried out farther and farther from the ship. Each wave became an eternity in which the captain could be seen on the top of one wave only to disappear into the trough of another.

SCs were equipped with a wherry with a lightweight outboard motor, and two men of the 656 wasted no time preparing to lower it. They were on the weather side and the wherry kept smashing against the side of the ship. One man, Charlie Adler, was already in the wherry when suddenly a large wave struck, tearing it free from the ship. White-faced, Charlie attempted to start the outboard but gave up after several tries and began rowing in an attempt to reach the captain. The crew members watched as Charlie, seemingly rowing in air on the crest of a wave, then completely disappearing in the trough of the next, made little headway.

The OD was finally able to maneuver the ship toward the captain, who had managed to get hold of one of the life rings. A cargo net was lowered, and he clambered up to where they could grab him and bring him aboard. He was sputtering mad, calling his crew a "bunch of goddamned fools" while they were recovering Charlie and the wherry. After a trip below to his cabin to change into dry clothes, Lieutenant O'Donnell reappeared and called everyone to quarters. He apologized for losing his composure and told the men they had done a remarkably creditable job under very difficult conditions.

Henry Rivers, the boatswain's mate who tells this story many years later, says it is not intended to be derogatory; in his opinion, Lieutenant O'Donnell was one of the finest persons with whom he served during five and a half years in the navy.

No sailor dreads anything more than a collision at sea, and subchaser men were especially aware of the threat of collision. Because of their small size, SCs were very difficult to spot in heavy seas. AB mentioned earlier, in some conditions they rode so low in the water that they looked startlingly like submarines and this, of course, was an open invitation for an attack from friendly ships. Near Alligator Reef off the Florida coast one night, PC 1123 mistook SC 1470 for a submarine, rammed it, and cut it almost in half. She was only doing what she had been trained to do. Her aggressive attack was her best defense against what she perceived to be a surfaced sub.

In a similar incident with a better ending, SC 989 was escorting a convoy one bright moonlit night from Key West to Guantanamo, maintaining position off the starboard bow of the convoy. The radioman overheard a message from one of the ships to all others in the convoy, announcing that there was a submarine off the starboard bow. The ships had mistaken the 989's low silhouette for a submarine and were talking about blowing it out of the water. The men on the beleaguered 989 spent a good portion of the night frantically trying to convince the convoy who they were.

The collision that Marion C. Bonham tells about was characteristically unpredictable. He had no sooner come aboard SC 1330 as its new executive officer when the ship was assigned to escort several vessels taking the Duke of Windsor, who was the governor of the Bahamas at the time, and his entourage back to the Bahamas after a visit to the United

States. The convoy consisted of a large group of ships. Among the escorts was an eighty-three foot Coast Guard patrol vessel, USCG 83421. At some time during the first evening out, John Winter, commanding officer, relieved Bonham of the watch and told him to go below and get some sleep. The weather was good, sea calm, visibility good.

Bonham had just taken off his pants, ready to jump into his bunk, when he felt the ship hit something, making a loud crashing sound. Pulling his pants back on, he rushed topside to observe the bow of the CG 83421 close aboard and perpendicular, with men clinging to it. The 1330 had plowed straight into it.

No ships were allowed to turn on their running lights and no search-lights were used during the rescue. Tight security had to be maintained, for there were U-boats in the area and the Prince of Wales was an important personage. The 1330 went alongside the unlucky vessel, pulled the men off, and brought them on board. All were saved, and none were happy. Although damage to the 1330 was relatively slight, the CG 83421 was cut in two about ten feet from the stern. A board of inquiry was held, but the cause of the collision was not clear and no one was ever blamed or held responsible for it. Lieutenant Winter remained in command of the 1330 to participate with valor at Utah Beach in the Normandy invasion a year later.

A collision nightmare came true at 2130 on the night of 2 March 1943. Escorting a convoy southbound off Cape Hatteras, SC 682 was patrolling her assigned station on the starboard quarter of the convoy. Conditions were poor, with a heaving cross sea and a northeasterly wind, intermittent squalls, and rain. Visibility had closed to about four hundred yards. The watch on the 682 was startled when, almost simultaneously, a broad line of running lights suddenly showed from ships unexpectedly approaching from the opposite direction. In those days of complete blackouts, nothing but the gravest emergency would cause ships to light their running lights. The lights were only six thousand yards ahead and closing fast. The unthinkable had happened. Two convoys, one southbound and the other northbound, were in the same shipping lane and on a collision course. Disaster was imminent.

Unable to determine what, if any, avoidance course her convoy was making, the 682 maintained her own course of 197 (T [true]). Suddenly a white flare fired by one of the northbound vessels was seen dead ahead. General quarters was sounded. Two lights were observed burning brightly near the waterline of what turned out to be a non-navy tug in trouble, the *Wellfleet*, while another larger vessel was lying to near the scene. John Gay, commanding officer of the 682, changing courses and speeds to avoid another northbound vessel, finally reached the scene and circled the *Wellfleet*, which appeared to be in a sinking condition. They could see a sizable hole at the waterline on the starboard side, and she was listing about 20 degrees. Clouds of steam billowed from a broken line. Signaling, the 682 asked if she needed assistance, to which the reply was affirmative.

The ship lying to about two hundred yards away was the merchant tanker *Edward L. Doheny*, and it was she who had struck the tug. The *Doheny* was in the act of lowering a boat when she signaled the 682 to ask if she could remove the men from the tug. In raging seas and sizable waves, Gay spent the next twenty-five minutes in a masterpiece of ship handling during which all seventeen men of the *Wellfleet* were transferred onto the 682 with no injuries and only minor damage to the 682. Detaching herself from the convoy, she proceeded to Morehead City, North Carolina, where she landed the men from the tug.

A survival story should have a happy ending, but, tragically, it would not be so for SC 1024, a sister escort in the 682's convoy. At the time the two convoys headed into each other on their collision courses, SC 1024 had been on her station, which was on the port quarter of the southbound convoy, some distance abeam the 682—both subchasers in the same relative position with respect to the convoy but on opposite sides.

Not until she arrived in Morehead City did the 682 learn that SC 1024 was missing. An air-sea rescue search was under way in the vicinity of the two-convoy collision. The search continued for several days but nothing, not a single trace, was ever found. SC 1024 had been swallowed up in the tumultuous sea, disappearing from the face of the earth without anyone knowing what happened to her.

Although the disappearance of the 1024 remains a mystery, another collision of ships among those two ill-fated convoys is the likeliest explanation. A tanker, SS *Cities Service Fuel*, or a merchant ship, SS *Plymouth*, in the northbound convoy, could have been involved, but exactly how is not clear. Each of the bigger ships reported that they thought they had hit something.

One can only imagine the horror of a giant steel bow cresting high on a wave and plunging down directly onto the subchaser in the trough below, driving it into the depths. Or perhaps, like a one-two punch, the big ships struck the 1024 in rapid succession, the first ship crushing the tiny subchaser into a helpless mass, followed by the second ship dealing the knockout blow, plunging her into oblivion. Whatever happened, the 1024 was hit so hard, so quickly, and so completely that she was destroyed and obliterated forever. By the time anyone on the tanker or merchant ship realized they might have hit something, it was all over. There were no survivors, no flotsam, no debris. Thirty miles off Cape Hatteras, SC 1024 and her twenty-five men vanished forever. The men of SC 1024 gave their lives for their country in a sudden, savage, inexplicable moment—as much a mystery now as then—on the high seas.

Nothing appeared in the papers about the missing subchaser until nine days later, when the *New York Times* published its weekly list of war casualties. The country was at war, and information of this type was routinely withheld because the military considered it too sensitive. Included in a little squib in the *Times'* weekly list of missing military and naval personnel from New Jersey appeared the name, "IRWIN, HERBERT, Jr., lieutenant, reserve; wife, Mrs. Sheila Saxton Irwin, Summit." Lieutenant Irwin was the commanding officer of SC 1024.

There being no proof of any drowning, the name of every man aboard SC 1024 had to be carried on the rolls of the Bureau of Naval Personnel as "missing" for one year, to conform with the Missing Persons Act. The legal uncertainty could only have prolonged the distress of their families. As a tribute to their sacrifice, and with deepest respect, the names of these men are listed below.

Herbert M. Irwin Jr., Lieutenant, USNR, Commanding Officer
Warren Williams Jr., Ensign, USNR, Executive Officer
George H. Guy, Ensign, USNR, Third Officer
John W Ahern, Machinist's Mate 2c, USNR
Thomas E. Bailey, Gunner's Mate 2c, USN
Adam Belich, Seaman 2c, USN
Curtis L. Bucklin, Motor Machinist's Mate 2c, USN
Gaetano Carusone, Ship's Cook 3c V-6, USNR
Chester J. Chapman, Radioman 3c V-6, USNR
Charles R. David, Fireman's Mate lc, USN
Albert H. Dow, Radioman 2c V-3, USNR
John A. Gilliam, Machinist's Mate 2c, USN
Harold V. Haner, Chief Boatswain's Mate (AA), USN
Joseph T. Lewandowski, Yeoman 3c V-6, USNR
Charles F. Liney, Apprentice Seaman V-6, USNR
Robert W McCommons, Gunner's Mate 3c V-6, USNR
Bennie F. McCurry, Seaman 2c, USN
Paul Olivieri, Apprentice Seaman V-6, USNR
George A. Pearson, Fireman's Mate lc M-2, USNR
George A. Perkins, Quartermaster 3c V-6, USNR
Louis B. Rieffel, Sonarman 3c V-6, USNR
Ellis E. Rudy, Sonarman 3c V-6, USNR
Ray C. Spicer, Mess Attendant 2c V-6, USNR
William H. Stopp, Electrician's Mate 2c V-6, USNR
Joseph E. Taylor, Sonarman 3c V-6, USNR

9 "Future of the Naval Reserve"

Captain Paul P. Blackburn, USN (Ret.)

U.S. Naval Institute *Proceedings*
(March 1945): 303–9

IMMEDIATELY AFTER the war ends, the Navy Department will be faced with the problems of the demobilization, and with the future of the Naval Reserve. The problems cannot be minimized, nor will it be easy to find the answers unless adequate plans are made before the victory is won. With over 90 per cent of the officers and 95 per cent of the enlisted men now on active duty subject to demobilization, discharge, or transfer to inactive duty within six months after the war ends, it becomes apparent that a chaotic Personnel situation can be avoided only by careful consideration of the interests of the men, and women, who are making victory certain, and by weighing their personal desires with the exigencies that may face the country.

In this connection, we must also consider the enlisted men of the regular services, many of whose enlistments have been extended for the duration of the war. These men will merit the same treatment as the members of the Naval Reserve and those brought into the Navy through Selective Service.

Twice within a generation it has been necessary for the Navy to expand many fold from its small regular force to meet the emergencies of a major war. The Navy has gone back once to a peace-time basis, and it is to be hoped that a second reduction to such an establishment will take place in the not-too distant future.

Those who remember the dislocations and inefficiencies that attended the demobilization of 1918–19 and the sad state to which the Navy was brought in the early 1920's as a result of various factors will hope that planning and, if necessary, legislation to obviate such conditions will be sufficiently advanced before this war comes to its successful conclusion. Only those who have gone through the period of transition from war to peace realize that this period is more complex and troublesome than going to war. As of November 9, 1918, the Navy consisted of 32,474 officers and 497,030 men, of which number 32 per cent of the officers and 40 per cent of the men were regulars; in October of 1944, there were about eight times as many officers and six times as many men, with a very much lower percentage of regulars. The number is still increasing and the percentage of regulars is dropping as officers and men continue to be added to meet war needs. Under the law as it now stands, the officers and men of the Naval Reserve are obligated to serve on active duty in time of war or during a national emergency; while a state of war, technically, continues until peace is declared, the war will be assumed by the country to have ended when fighting ceases.

As the Secretary of the Navy stated in his annual report for the fiscal year 1919:

Scarcely had the armistice been signed when the young men who had served so well looked eagerly to return to the pursuits of peace, and only the sense of duty held them until the soldiers who had won glory in France could be brought back home in transports manned by the Navy. . . . There was danger of the Navy going stale in 1919–1920 as it had gone stale following every other war.

How stale it went in the two years after World War I is indicated in the Secretary's report of 1922:

> The Atlantic Fleet . . . has performed only the routine work incident to target practice and engineering competitions. There were no combined maneuvers on account of lack of appropriations. . . . The Pacific Fleet . . . operated from San Pedro, California, except during the summer months. Limited appropriations confined the operations of this fleet to routine target practice and engineering competitions.

The personnel situation was at its worst during 1919–20, when the "duration-of-the war" enlisted men were being discharged at such a rapid rate that there were insufficient experienced men to operate the ships. In order to equalize conditions between regular Navy, reserves, and those who had enlisted for the war, all were considered to have enlisted for the duration; wages in civil life were good, jobs ashore were plentiful, and there was the natural tendency to get out of uniform. All of these factors influenced most of the men in the Navy to accept their discharges.

In his annual report for the fiscal year 1920, dated December 1, 1920, the Secretary of the Navy reported:

> The transition period since the war has been a trying time for the Navy, and that it has been successfully weathered is a subject for congratulation. First came demobilization, with the discharge not only of the hundreds of thousands who had enlisted for the war, but also of thousands of regulars who, having completed their terms of service, were unwilling to re-enlist unless they were assured of an increase of pay somewhat commensurate with what they would get in civil life. . . . Because of the demobilization and better financial opportunities in civil life, the task of securing recruits has been difficult and expensive, but this is a temporary condition which always follows war.

The Secretary goes on to say further:

The Naval Reserve force today (December 1, 1920) comprises approximately 28,000 officers and 227,000 men. This constitutes a vast source of naval strength upon which we may draw in any emergency, and its encouragement and maintenance must always demand the utmost consideration. . . . We would be recreant to our duty did we not take every possible step to promote their welfare and retain their connection with and interest in the service.

It may be of interest to explore the twenty years following this report to learn what steps were taken to encourage and maintain this "vast source of naval strength" and to "retain their connection with and interest in the service."

The Naval Reserve had been created by the Act of August 29, 1916, as the Naval Reserve Force, consisting of six classes, viz.: Naval Reserve, Naval Auxiliary Reserve, Naval Coast Defense Reserve, Volunteer Naval Reserve, Naval Reserve Flying Corps. This act superseded the provisions of the appropriation act for the fiscal year 1916 (Act of March 3, 1915), which created a United States Naval Reserve of men honorably discharged after one or more terms of enlistment. No provision had been made in the appropriation act for officers, nor for the enrollment of those who had had no previous service. The only civilians with training for the Navy were in the Naval Militia units, essentially state organizations.

Minor changes in the laws governing the Naval Reserve were enacted during World War I, by which the officers and men of the Naval Militia became successively National Naval Volunteers and, on July 1, 1918, members of the U.S. Naval Reserve Force.

Under the requirements of war the Navy expanded from its July 1, 1916, strength of 4,293 officers and 54,234 men to the total, on November 9, 1918, of 32,474 officers and 497,030 men, of which numbers

68 percent of the officers and 60 per cent of the men were in the Naval Reserve Force.

The Naval Appropriations Act approved June 4, 1920, carried authorization for (a) employment of not to exceed 20,000 enlisted reservists with their own consent to serve on active duty for not less than twelve months or more than eighteen months; (b) employment of 500 reserve officers in aviation and auxiliary service; (c) transfer to permanent line ranks and grades of 1,200 temporary commissioned and warrant officers of Navy and Naval Reserve Forces upon qualification to the rank, not above lieutenant, for which they were found qualified; (d) transfer of a proportionate number of staff officers to the regular Navy.

At the end of June, 1921, the Naval Reserve Force gave continuing promise of normal existence with its 26,376 officers and 203,666 men. Estimates of $12,000,000 for retainer pay and active duty pay were submitted to Congress, but "Economy!" had become the watchword, and the appropriation for the Naval Reserve for the fiscal year 1922 was $7,000,000. By the end of September the entire appropriation was expended or obligated. This left the Navy Department no option except to transfer 25,000 officers and about 200,000 men to the Volunteer Naval Reserve, members of which serve without pay, or to disenroll them.

Accordingly, all members of the Naval Reserve Force except members of the Fleet Naval Reserve and of the Volunteer Naval Reserve were disenrolled, with very few exceptions. At the end of the fiscal year, June 30, 1922, the Naval Reserve Force had been reduced to 5,340 officers and 10,966 men.

Within the next few years came the period of retrenchment in expenditures; the United States was committed to a limitation of armaments, the pacifist element was growing in strength and power, and interest in naval and military affairs was at a low ebb. The Naval Reserve Force became the "redheaded stepchild" of the Navy Department, which was fighting desperately to retain at least a nucleus of a regular Navy. Congress, responsive to the expressed will of the people, kept naval appropriations at a minimum; there was then no war in sight so there seemed no reason to encourage and maintain the "vast source of naval strength" inherent in the 300,000 men absorbed into the civil population after their valuable war service in the Navy.

New legislation to provide for the Naval Reserve and Marine Corps Reserve, and designed as a substitute for earlier laws on the subject, was prepared by the Navy Department and introduced in Congress on March 27, 1922, but did not become a law until February 28, 1925, when it was approved by the President. This legislation, known as "An act providing for the creation, organization, administration, and maintenance of a Naval Reserve and a Marine Corps Reserve," went into effect on July 1, 1925.

The principal features of this law (a) transferred all members of the Naval Reserve Force and the Marine Corps Reserve, respectively, to the Naval Reserve and the Marine Corps Reserve; (b) tenure of office of officers was during the pleasure of the President; (c) preserved benefits of continuous service to men enlisting in the reserve within three months of discharge from the Navy; (d) safeguarded interests of transferred members of the Fleet Naval Reserve; and (e) provided for additional classes to be known as Merchant Marine Naval Reserve and Volunteer Reserve.

The years 1923, 1924, 1925, and 1926 saw little change in the activities of the Naval Reserve. It was in the doldrums and was kept alive largely through the interest and effort of a group of men who had made naval training a lifetime hobby. Training cruises were arranged for the units of the then Fleet Naval Reserve, and there was authorization for drill pay as well as for subsistence while on week-end cruises.

By June 30, 1926, the Reserve had recovered from the knockdown blow of 1922 only to the extent of having an enrollment of 3,736 officers and 18,868 men, plus 7,173 sixteen- and twenty-year fleet reservists.

For the next twelve years, i.e., from 1926 to 1938, the Naval Reserve drifted along with no very great change in its status. Boards, from time to time, were convened to consider Naval Reserve matters and to recommend new legislation. The Naval Affairs Committee of the House appointed a select committee to frame a new Naval Reserve law in January, 1936, but the committee made no recommendation. The Navy Department sponsored the draft of a bill in March, 1937, but the Bureau of the Budget deemed it not in harmony with the President's program at that time.

Finally, on May 6, 1938, the Secretary of the Navy transmitted to the Speaker of the House of Representatives "a draft of a proposed bill to provide for the creation, organization, administration, and maintenance of a Naval Reserve and a Marine Corps Reserve" and recommended its enactment. Hearings were held, and in these it was brought out that the Naval Reserve then consisted of:

Fleet Naval Reserve Officers	1,170
Merchant Marine Naval Reserve Officers	3,602
Volunteer Naval Reserve Officers	7,387
Total	12,159
Fleet Naval Reserve Enlisted Men	9,863
Merchant Marine Naval Reserve Enlisted Men	79
Volunteer Naval Reserve Enlisted Men	12,738
Total	122,680
Fleet Naval Reserve Transferred Men	15,760

With certain modifications, the draft submitted by the Secretary of the Navy became "The Naval Reserve Act of 1938" and is still the basic law governing the Naval Reserve, a component part of the United States Navy. This law provided for (a) the Fleet Reserve of men who had had sixteen or twenty years' active naval service; (b) the Organized Reserve of officers and men attached to active units required to attend drills; (c) the Merchant Marine Reserve; (d) the Volunteer Naval Reserve; and (e) the Marine Corps Reserve.

All reservists now on duty are serving under the provision of the Naval Reserve Act of 1938 that:

Any member of the Naval Reserve, including those on the honorary retired list . . . may be ordered to active duty by the Secretary of the Navy in time of war or when, in the opinion of the President, a national emergency exists, and may be required to perform active duty throughout the war or until the national emergency ceases to exist.

This same act authorizes the Secretary of the Navy to "release any member [of the Naval Reserve] from active duty either in time of war or in time of peace."

Published estimates as to naval personnel, including Marine Corps and Coast Guard, indicate that the total will approximate 3,500,000 by June 30, 1945. Demobilization of the Navy at the end of World War II, therefore, involves about six times as many individuals as were affected in 1919.

In the consideration of the action to be taken to insure an adequate reserve for the future, and to avoid the many personnel troubles that plagued the Navy during the 1920's, a realistic approach to the next ten years is essential.

Two basic factors will govern the enlisted and officer strength of the Navy in the next decade. First, how many men will be required to man the ships, aircraft, and stations that must be kept in commission to accomplish the tasks that become the obligations of the United States in the post-war years? Second, how much money will the people of the United States appropriate annually for the military establishment, Army and Navy, including air arms?

It is assumed that officers and men of the Coast Guard will resume their regular duties, and that reduction of Coast Guard personnel will be the responsibility of the Commandant of that organization. Combatant ships now Coast Guard manned will either be placed out of commission or will be manned by Navy crews. Reduction of the Marine Corps to a peacetime basis affects the Navy demobilization because funds for the Marines are included in Naval Appropriations Acts, and because the strength of the Corps is based on naval requirements. No attempt will be made in this paper to estimate future requirements for the Marine Corps; it is sufficient to say that our bases in the Atlantic and the Pacific will need many more Marines than were in the service prior to 1940.

From the war strength of three million, exclusive of Coast Guard and Marine Corps, it will be necessary to retain a minimum of 500,000 officers and men on active duty in the Navy to meet our obligations under any organization that may be set up for the maintenance of world peace and world order. Will half a million of the three million now in the Navy be willing to accept permanent status in the Navy when peace treaties become effective?

On the basis of experience after the last war, there will be only a few who are willing to continue in the Navy besides officers of the regular Navy, petty officers of the regular Navy with eight or more years of service, and a small percentage of reservists. Service in the Navy in peacetime is a business; in wartime, service is a patriotic duty. A slogan like "Your Navy Needs You!" has little appeal unless the man to whom the slogan is directed needs the Navy. Service must therefore be made attractive if the postwar Navy is to be manned by volunteers to the extent necessary for post-war obligations.

There can be little prospect, nor is there a need, to keep the post-war Navy manned on a war basis. As in this war, most of the personnel for any future war must come from the Naval Reserve; we will have the ships and may have learned from the lessons of the last twenty-five years the futility of disarmament. If the lesson has been learned, ships will be scrapped only as they become obsolete and are replaced by modern units.

How can we be assured of a Naval Reserve competent and adequate in number to commission ships in "storage" and to fill the billets ashore?

Much of the pre-war organization of the Naval Reserve, as developed during the period of the renaissance between 1938 and 1941, appears sound and should be renewed. Since the primary consideration is provision of trained personnel, the Bureau of Personnel is the logical agency of the Navy Department to have supervision and control of all Naval Reserve matters.

Under the Chief of Naval Personnel should be a rear admiral or senior captain, U.S. Navy, who is conversant with and cognizant of reserve problems, requirements, and capabilities, with the title of Director of the Naval Reserve. Assistants from the Navy and from major subdivisions of the reserve should be assigned to the office of the Director; there will be a natural rotation of directors and regular officers assigned to the division, but there should be a policy that limits reserve officers to four years of duty with the Director. A Naval Reserve Inspection Board, under the Chief of Naval Operations and composed entirely of regular officers, will keep fully employed inspecting units of the Naval Reserve.

In each Naval District, there should be a Director of the Naval Reserve (regular Navy) and an Assistant Director (Naval Reserve). The Assistant Director will be limited to four years of active duty in the District, but may have an additional period of the same length in the Naval Reserve Division of the Bureau of Naval Personnel. Sufficient assistants and instructors for administration, procurement, enlistments, discharges, records, etc., will be essential in each Naval District; these may be either regulars or Naval Reserve. A minimum allowance of officers for a District Naval Reserve Headquarters includes:

Captain, U.S.N., as Director, Naval Reserve; Captain or Commander, U.S.N.R., as Assistant Director; Commander, U.S.N., as Training Officer. As Assistants to Training Officer and Instructors (Instructors to be assigned to specific battalions) there should be 5 Line Lieutenants, U.S.N.; 5 Line Lieutenants, U.S.N.R.; 1 Medical Officer; 1 Civil Engineer; 2 Communications Officers; 5 Naval Aviators (U.S.N. or 1 WAVE Officer); and a Clerical Group of U.S.N., U.S.N.R., and Civil Service employees.

A weakness of the old Organized Reserve was the shortage of instructors; with the proposed enlarged reserve, there will be fulltime jobs for as many instructors as can be made available. Rotation of duty between the fleet and the Naval Reserve should prevent stagnation of ideas and keep Naval Reserve training abreast of fleet ideas.

The division of the Naval Reserve into (a) Fleet, (b) Organized, (c) Volunteer, and (d) Merchant Marine sections was a logical subdivision, but did not work out too well, largely because we got into the war by stages instead of in the way our planners had visualized our entry. The Fleet Reserve of 16- and 20-year men had an effective percentage of about fifty when we needed these men and called them to duty; too many were physically disqualified for any service, and many more were fit for shore duty only. The Organized Reserves were first called on a volunteer basis, which disrupted the divisions, and then were ordered by divisions to transports, cargo ships, or other types of vessels, instead of to the destroyers for which they had been specially trained. The Volunteer Reserve lacked training and was little better indoctrinated than the civilian who had had no previous connection with the Navy. The Merchant Marine had almost no enlisted men, and the ranks held by Merchant Marine officers bore little relation to the capabilities of these officers; when war was declared many Merchant Marine Reserve officers who did not volunteer for active duty remained on an inactive status to draw war zone pay, while their contemporaries, also operating in war zones, were paid from the much lower Navy pay table.

Organized Reserve.—In order to carry on systematic training for those whose residence, circumstances, and interest in the naval service make regular attendance at drills practicable, it is desirable that the Organized Reserve be reestablished and enlarged. Naval Reserve armories now converted to other use should be rehabilitated and armories provided where none exist. Destroyer escorts and frigates assigned to battalions will promote morale. Certainly, a minimum strength of 5,000 line officers, 5,000 staff officers, and 100,000 men should be trained and immediately available during the period when plans for permanent peace in the world have not had time to demonstrate their enduring efficacy. All branches of the Navy need representation in the Organized Reserve, and the following might well be the organization in one of the populous naval districts:

- 30 Battalions, of 500 enlisted men (and women) each
- 20—Ship's Company, comprising Deck, Engineer, Communications, Supply, Commissary, Medical
- 4—Aviation, with ground personnel
- 4—Amphibious, with landing craft operating and repair personnel, construction companies, field communicators, etc.
- 2—Hospital, complete with nurses, corpsmen, technicians, specialists, etc. (for a major base hospital).

Specialist groups within some of the appropriate battalions should be formed for training in mine warfare, combat intelligence, photography and photographic interpretation, underwater defenses and detection, and aerology, to name a few of the many distinctive lines of naval endeavor.

Officers and men of the battalions will be members of the Organized Reserve, will have an allowance for uniforms, will be paid for attendance at drills, and will be required to perform two weeks' training duty, with pay, annually. The Navy will have the obligation to furnish suitable instruction, adequate instructional material, and an opportunity for the training period. If these men are sufficiently interested in preparing themselves for useful service in the Navy, the United States can adopt a pinch-penny attitude that will make this preparation insufficient. The Organized Reserve has no justification unless it is composed of officers and enlisted personnel able to go to duty without delay, and able to perform the duties of their ranks or ratings with a minimum of further training.

Many details of the organization and training need to be worked out. The good features of the prewar Organized Reserve should be retained, and results of our experience during the war can be applied as practicable. Planning is essential and should not be deferred up to the moment when action becomes necessary. In this connection, it is noted from the press that the War Department has appointed a board of officers to draw up plans for the reserve components of the Army.

Fleet Reserve.—The Fleet Reserve will comprise the fully trained men who have had sixteen or twenty years, or more, in the Navy. Those who are physically qualified for duty are immediately available to perform the duties of their ratings, and experience in this war has taught us the value of these "old-timers." In 1940–41 this group was a disappointment to some officers in the Navy Department who had insufficient knowledge as to the general qualifications, physical, mental, moral, and professional, of the men after varying periods of inactive duty. Provision for a biennial physical examination of all men in this category will keep current an accurate estimate of the availability of the 16- and 20-year men for active duty. Since most of the 16-year men will have completed 20 years before the end of the war, and few others who enlisted originally before July 1, 1925, will have less than 20 years, practically all of our Fleet Reservists will have had at least 20 years of service, and all who transfer in the post-war years will be in the 20-year group.

The basic law provides for the enrollment in the Fleet Reserve of regular officers who have resigned from the service, but this provision of the law was invoked in very few instances. It would be desirable to accept for enrollment as Fleet Reservists those regular officers who resign under honorable conditions. Special inducements might be offered to them if they keep themselves professionally qualified for the duties of their ranks.

Volunteer Reserve.—The greater portion of men and women released from active duty at the end of the war will be faced with the necessity of getting and holding jobs, completing their educations, reestablishing themselves in their homes and communities, and readjusting themselves to civil life. Most of them will not be in a position to attend regular drills or classes, either because of lack of desire, or want of opportunity. At the same time, they may wish to retain their connection with the Navy, and surely the Navy should wish to retain their interest and co-operation.

Into the Volunteer Reserve should go the hundreds of thousands of men and women who have served their country well in the trying war years. If it is apparent that the Naval Reserve is to be a militant vital organization with good leadership, adequate support from the Navy Department, and a definite program, the response from the personnel now carrying on afloat and ashore should be good.

The following plan is suggested for discussion and consideration:

(a) Upon discharge or release to inactive duty, under honorable conditions and if physically qualified, all enlisted men and women are afforded the opportunity to enroll in the Volunteer Naval Reserve for four years, with the option of transferring to the Organized Reserve in their home districts.

(b) All enlisted personnel will be enrolled in the ratings held by them.

(c) Officers will have the same rank in the Naval Reserve as their running mates who remain in the regular Navy. Ranks are to be adjusted within two years after the war ends.

(d) Officers and enlisted personnel will be required to submit a report to District Commandants annually, giving pertinent data as to address, next of kin, employment, special skills or attainments, etc.

(e) Qualified personnel will be enrolled as officers or enlisted men in appropriate ranks or ratings by Directors of Naval Reserve in the various districts.

(f) Officers will be eligible for promotion with their running mates in the regular Navy, but must qualify for the higher rank by examination within one year after they have been notified that they are eligible. Those who fail to qualify will be disenrolled.

(g) Since all inductees through Selective Service are, by law, members of the Naval Reserve for ten years after the end of the war, these men will be considered a part of the Volunteer Reserve unless they enlist in the Navy or join a unit of the Organized Reserve.

(h) Retainer Pay of $20 will be paid annually to all members of the Volunteer Reserve who comply with paragraph (d) above (i.e., submit the annual report).

Merchant Marine Reserve.—Reestablishment of the Merchant Marine Reserve on a peacetime basis will be more complicated than for any other branch of the Naval Reserve. There are now two distinct groups of officers trained in the Merchant Marine. One group is on active duty in the Navy, and in this group officers have been promoted to higher rank with other officers of the Navy. The other group has served with the Merchant Marine throughout the war but has had no increase in naval rank, though most of these men have been promoted in the services of the companies for whom they sail. An additional complication is the issuance of appointments with naval titles to officers of the Maritime Service who hold Naval Reserve commissions in lower ranks or have resigned from the Naval Reserve.

Hundreds of new officers have been trained for the merchant service and are commissioned in the Maritime Service or in the Naval Reserve. In the interest of uniformity, it is considered highly desirable that all officers of the U.S. Merchant Marine be appointed or commissioned in one service; from the standpoint of availability for war, the Merchant Marine Naval Reserve should be that one.

The enlistment of Merchant Marine unlicensed personnel in a special class of the Naval Reserve offers no advantages. In time of war the expansion of the Merchant Marine will require more men than will be available.

Naval Reserve Officers' Training Corps.—Continuation of the N.R.O.T.C. in colleges and universities is the best method of providing young officers for the Naval Reserve.

Conclusion.—The reestablishment and continuation of the Naval Reserve after the war require advance planning. A policy prepared and accepted with a reasonable assurance that it will govern the transition from war to peace, and that it will carry on during the foreseeable future, is essential if we are to profit by the hard lessons of the last twenty-five years. This time let us hope that we shall be more successful in our effort to "retain the connection with and interest in the service" of this "vast source of naval strength."

A Graduate of the Naval Academy in the class of 1904, **Captain Blackburn** saw active service in various grades and on numerous ships and stations until he was retired in 1939. He was recalled to active duty in September, 1939, as Director of the Naval Reserve, 3d Naval District.

"Standby Squadron"

10

Lieutenant W. H. Vernor Jr., USNR

U.S. Naval Institute *Proceedings*
(July 1952): 729–39

IF YOU'VE EVER DRIVEN between the Texas cities of Fort Worth and Dallas on a Sunday morning, chances are you've seen some of the rugged, old Navy TBM torpedo bombers lumbering into the air from Dallas' nearby Naval Air Station. You've seen these planes on weekends because they've been turned over to the Navy's Air Reserves, civilians who use their weekends to renew their proficiency in the art of flying and keep up with the latest developments in Naval Aviation. These air reserves, many of them Navy veterans, have maintained more than a nodding acquaintance with the Navy over the past few years. Not only at Dallas, but at other similar Naval Air Stations scattered over the nation, these Sunday flying reserves have become known as the "Weekend Warriors."

This program was set up by foresighted regular Navy airmen at high command levels. Since the end of the last war, it has kept available a trained and ready pool of organized squadrons—at a fraction of the cost required to maintain a large, continuously active air arm. When fighting broke out in Korea, certain of these standby squadrons were quickly activated; the practical test of the plan was underway. And now that several air groups of these all-reserve squadrons have been operating from aircraft carriers off Korea for many months, the test results are clear: the Navy's "Weekend Warrior" plan has paid off.

The Sudden Call

Among those units selected for sudden activation was Attack Squadron 702, one of several reserve units based at N.A.S. Dallas. All over Dallas that evening of July 20, 1950, telephones began to ring in earnest, and the calls continued well into the night. The wire services picked up some government business contacting those members of Squadron 702 who could not be reached by telephone. Teams of Navy and Marine personnel set about combing the city to inform hard-to-reach squadron members. Lights burned late that night at the air station.

Typical of the enlisted members called was a certain aviation engine mechanic whose civilian job was right in line with his air reserve duties. He was a mechanic for Pioneer Air Lines at Dallas' Love Field, so it was logical that he was an important crew member of the squadron's maintenance organization. He was just getting settled down in a new home, and Navy records had not caught up with his change of address. Efforts to reach him during the day had failed, and he worked on in blissful ignorance of the changes being wrought in his future. His only inkling of the impending call was a terse item he saw in the afternoon papers, stating that an undesignated Navy reserve squadron was being activated.

That evening, he stopped by the Pioneer hangar to have a Coke and a chat with the boys on the night shift. News of the recall was bandied about at some length, but he dismissed the idea with the suggestion that it must have been another unit; he went on to take his family to a drive-in theater. Meanwhile, the Navy was getting hot on his trail, and at one the following morning, a Navy team appeared at the Pioneer hangar looking for him. He was at home, enjoying the sleep of a peaceful citizen. With some consideration, the representatives left word for him to report the next morning!

Within 48 hours, some eighty enlisted men, twenty pilots, and four ground officers of the squadron had reported in at the Dallas Naval Air Station. Some even came all the way from Sweetwater, out in West Texas, and Tulsa, Oklahoma; others came from the distant towns of Kilgore, Longview, and Corpus Christi. A dispatch bristled up the chain of command, reporting Attack Squadron 702 mobilized and ready for further assignment. At higher levels, plans were already well made. The unit was given a few more days at Dallas to prepare for continuous active duty. At the station, there was much activity. Records had to be completed and brought up to date, gear, files and publications were packed, clothing was issued, and everyone received physical examinations and the inevitable inoculations. . . . Pay records, allotments, wills, powers of attorney, and government insurance were among other numerous details that had to be taken care of.

The effects on the personal lives of the men called up were obviously far-reaching and, in some cases, violent. Everyone had his own personal affairs to wind up and set in order, and only a few days to do it in. Civilian jobs and businesses were set aside or discontinued. Family living arrangements were shuffled about and changed; homes were sold, rented, or closed up. Careers were sidetracked. New financial problems were created which were not easily solved—for all, the call to active duty meant considerable personal sacrifice.

The Squadron Moves West

After a week of hectic preparation the unit was ready to move. Navy transport planes, loaded with the entire complement, took off into the early dawn, headed west. Soon, these planes, manned by other reserves, were touching down at North Island, the Naval Air Station at San Diego, California. Headquarters for ComAirPac (Commander. Air Force, Pacific Fleet), this facility was to be the reserves' training base for a few months to follow.

That afternoon at North Island was a busy one as reserve-manned transports from many parts of the country flew in every few minutes. The accents varied from Midwestern to deep southern, but the look of the reserves was the same, as they piled in from Detroit, Chicago, Kansas City, New Orleans, Atlanta, Alameda, Los Angeles, Memphis, St. Louis, and other cities. Within only a few hours, newly-activated squadrons sufficient to man more than two large carrier air groups had been air-lifted, en masse, to the focal point at San Diego. This, in itself, was a striking demonstration of naval airpower!

Only the day before, the North Island air facility had been practically deserted—for the regular Navy air groups stationed there had been rushed forward to fire the first shots in the Navy's air war in Korea. Now, North Island again teemed with activity; two great hangars had been hung with large banners bearing the words, "Welcome Weekend Warriors!" To make the welcome more timely, the word "Weekend" had been painted over with a big red "X."

ComAirPac welcomed the reserves: "There's lots of work ahead of us. I want you to get yourselves settled and to relax. When the time comes for you to go forward, we want you to be as polished and as ready as we know how to make you. . . . I know you are all here at great personal sacrifice and I admire you all the more for it. Welcome to the team."

As the squadrons set about their refresher training in earnest, businesslike flights of Corsairs, Skyraiders, and Panthers became commonplace around San Diego. Squadron 702 pilots began "checking out" in the AD Skyraiders which replaced the rugged, but slow, old TBM Avengers. These new attack bombers were now fleet standard—bigger, faster, more powerful flying platforms for lifting tons of bombs and projectiles from decks of fast carriers at sea.

There was much work ahead. "Ordnance" men and electronicsmen attended service schools to study the new equipment built into the planes. Maintenance men and check crews worked day and night readying the new planes for service. Green plane captains were given the word on their duties. Pilots were also kept busy: at first, with lecture and classes, altitude indoctrination, instrument refreshers with Link trainer hops, and additional training in navigation and electronics. There were new tactics to be studied. As more planes became available, ground schools gave way to flight operations with instrument and navigation training, nightflying, gunnery, rocketry, dive and glide bombing, and close air support. There were days of "bounce drill" (Navy parlance for practice carrier landings on land), followed by real carrier landings at sea, along with division and group tactics. In short, everything possible was done to bring the veteran pilots up to date in all phases of their training, to put them on a par with regular Navy "ready" squadrons.

Seven Hundred Two Joins the Fight

The training days are long past now. In March, 1951 Attack Squadron 702 began flying from the decks of the U.S.S. *Boxer*, a 27,000 ton aircraft carrier. The *Boxer*'s air group was an all-reserve air group, the first carrier-based reserves to represent the Navy with United Nations forces in Korea. Snows still covered the ground in Korea when *Boxer* joined Navy Task Force 77, and her blue planes went right to work. In daily strikes against the enemy, three all-reserve fighter squadrons joined the Dallas Group flying from the *Boxer*'s decks. These units hailed from Olathe, Kansas; Glenview, Illinois; and Memphis, Tennessee. The appearance of *Boxer* and her air group in Korean waters meant that another fine aircraft carrier and her regular air group, which had been hitting hard at the enemy for many months, could return to the states for a well-deserved rest.

Navy Air over Korea

When the blue planes of Navy Task Force 17 appear over Korea, it is sometimes difficult to appreciate the efforts which put them there. Somewhere at sea, mighty ships, manned by thousands, exist for the sole purpose of launching these aircraft. Each individual in the great team comprising the fast carrier task force contributes to the effort, for the planes are the long range "guns" which enable the Navy to strike deep into the enemy heartland.

Long before dawn, ordnancemen on the carriers work in total or semi-darkness, hoisting heavy bombs and rockets onto the aircraft wing racks. Others operate carts which bring the loads up from the innards of the ship to the planes on the deck. During these same dark hours, "pushers" trundle the loaded aircraft aft on deck to complete the re-spot for the early morning launch. Planes are crowded together with wings folded and only inches to spare, for space, even on the largest of carriers, is always at a premium. Loaded planes must have every possible foot of deck run to struggle into the air with thousands of pounds of explosives.

Below decks, there is activity during every hour of the day. Technicians labor at many tasks: keeping engines in top shape, checking flight gear, tuning and maintaining electronic equipment, and repairing damaged aircraft. Hundreds of other members of the ship's company work at the myriad tasks of running the ship, which exists to support the air group and its mission. In the ready rooms, where pilots stand by before flights, there is also a hum of activity. Flight leaders and air intelligence officers brief pilots on the day's operations. Late navigational and weather data reach the ready rooms by teletype from the ship's communications centers. When a pilot leaves the ready room to man his aircraft, he carries a fund of the latest information needed to enable him to perform the mission.

The launch of aircraft is a critical period. When every ounce of available power is needed, engine failure during take-off usually means the loss of an airplane. In spite of every possible precaution, such failures sometimes occur. It is then that the ship's "angel" —the plane guard helicopter, always hovering near the carrier, can swoop down and pick up the wet, shaken pilot. Rescue of the pilot can be effected within seconds if a plane with a faltering engine "hits the drink."

Minutes after the first plane is aloft, the entire strike group is airborne. Remaining planes are moved or taxied about on deck to make room for the next launch or recovery. While this goes on, departing flight leaders rendezvous their planes while circling the force and the groups then proceed toward their target areas; returning flights "break up" their formations into the closely timed interval of the carrier landing pattern. Aircraft recovery aboard a carrier is one of the most striking demonstrations of teamwork, precision, and split-second timing to be seen in any naval operation. A smartly executed recovery brings eight to ten planes aboard in something like four minutes—spectators who have never before witnessed such a performance never fail to be impressed, and rightly so.

Over Korea, Navy carrier air missions fall into two general categories: close air support, and interdiction. Both are strictly tactical. The first contributes to the primary objective of UN forces in Korea: to kill as many of the enemy as possible. The purpose of the second is to keep the enemy from getting supplies and reinforcements to his front line forces.

Mass Annihilation

Close air support might better be termed mass annihilation. Fortunately, our front line forces have met with little enemy air opposition, and this has enabled our own tactical air to account for a staggering total of enemy casualties. The effect of close air support weapons is devastating; the fragmentation bombs and jellied gasoline (napalm) bombs have done much to help suppress the enemy's human sea tactics. When burning napalm does not actually contact enemy troops, it has been known to cause deaths by suffocation, since the fiercely burning liquid exhausts much of the oxygen from the surrounding atmosphere.

Air Force, Marine, and Navy air all combine talents at this mass annihilation. Under control of Air Force personnel, planes flying close air support drop their death-dealing loads wherever directed by these target seekers. The Air Force controllers themselves work in close contact with ground units which may call for air support as the tactical situation dictates. They direct the attacks of the close air support planes by radio, either from jeeps or from "mosquito" planes—light trainer or liaison type aircraft which can fly low over the terrain, seeking out the targets. Dense foliage, rugged terrain, and camouflage conceal enemy troops and gun positions, making it difficult, often impossible, to determine accurately the results of close air support attacks. Only when a known enemy gun position ceases fire, or after friendly troops move into an area and find enemy dead, are the true results known.

Once a group of Corsairs and Skyraiders from the *Boxer* worked several consecutive days over a stubborn enemy-held ridge near the 38th parallel. Their controller reported good coverage, but added that heavy enemy ground fire made it impossible to fly down close enough for an actual evaluation of results. On the final day of that action, the same group of *Boxer* planes returned to the area and was greeted by the controller with the news that friendly troops had taken the ridge during the night and had counted over a thousand enemy dead. This total, credited to close air support planes flying in that area, was an impressive demonstration of this use of tactical air.

Interdiction and the Bridge Busters

Sharing importance with the tasks of close air support, the mission of denying the enemy supplies and reinforcements also is a big job for carrier based Navy air. Breaking railroad and highway bridges is the primary part of this task; most of these installations in North Korea have taken a terrific pounding since the war began. Mountainous Korea offers many good bridge targets, and the enemy effort to move his supplies is severely strained by the loss of so many of these bridges. But the enemy is ingenious, patient, and unremittingly persistent. He may carefully nurse one supply trainload over the few miles of track between two broken bridges, unload and ferry the load across the break by pack animal, cart, or truck, reload it onto another train to traverse the next stretch of track to the next break, repeating this process until the destination is reached. When bad flying weather hampers the interdiction program, he works feverishly by day and night at repairing his routes and bridges, reconstructing and bypassing with amazing dispatch. Then the weather clears a bit, and the Navy's bridgebusters go at it again—the pilots have developed remarkable bombing accuracy, and there are few bridges in North Korea which have not suffered therefrom.

When the aircraft of a bridgebuster mission have finished off their target with heavy bombs, they continue to hammer at railroads and highway junctions with their remaining light bombs. A strike group will usually finish off a mission on armed reconnaissance—attention is given to seeking out "targets of opportunity," such as locomotives, rolling stock, trucks, tanks, pack animals, carts, troop concentrations, fuel, ammunition, and supply dumps. A skilled eye is needed to pick out vehicles and supplies concealed under foliage, straw, or refuse—the enemy is an ingenious camoufleur. Adroit at rapid concealment, he can often completely hide a vehicle after it has already been spotted from the air—in the space of time required for the pilot to maneuver into position to make a strafing run. This is often done by simply driving the vehicle through the side of any convenient house, until the vehicle is well under cover. If no suitable habitation is available in the vicinity, the next resort is to rapidly pile scrub brush and straw all around and over the vehicle. . . One pilot, attempting to describe the way a camouflaged vehicle appears from the air, commented, "Really, they look just like piles of rubbish." Pilots soon learned that many such innocent-looking rubbish piles respond to strafing by bursting into livid orange flame!

The Pilots

They come from many walks of life; nearly all are married men with families. Any one of them could have been your next door neighbor. Although most of the men are civilians at heart, they maintain a healthy spirit and capacity for getting the job done in the Navy. They are fully aware of their value to the Navy as aviators, and of their obligation to the government which spared no expense to make them the best aviators in the world.

Some of these reserves face a personal decision which is closely involved with the Navy: to remain reserve, and plan on getting back home to civilian pursuits again, or to go "regular," if and when the opportunity is presented. The average reserve has spent four or five years becoming established in the civilian world. In the sudden recall, he drops the civilian career by the wayside, and again takes up the exacting tasks for which the Navy trained him. His formidable array of awards and decorations represent years of naval experience which will be valuable to him if he stays on, as will the gradual accumulation of seniority. Yet there are those who find the demands of the naval career too far removed from civilian ways of life; they are ready and willing to join in the fight—but when their services are no longer needed, they want to be civilians again. And they may suffer a little from the fact that there are few civilian jobs which make use of the special talents the Navy has developed in them.

The older pilots may often joke about approaching the age when they should be put "out to pasture," but their record on this tour has certainly demonstrated that the younger pilots are not necessarily the best pilots. All these reserves go about the job with an unflagging enthusiasm, while the regular Navy people smile patiently and indulgently at their concern with the "when" of their return to inactive duty and civilian life.

Enemy Flak, Dangerous and Ever Present

Searching out the targets, either on close air support or interdiction missions, is no picnic for pilots. Enemy anti-aircraft defenses have multiplied tremendously since the war began. Pilots have to fly low, often too low for safety, to find cleverly hidden targets. A continuous compromise must be forced between flying low enough to find targets and presenting the enemy with a good target by flying too low. Naval airmen are advised by the Task Force Commander that no target in Korea is presently worth the life of a pilot. Yet, the toll on the enemy attests to the daring of these flyers, who are finding the targets, often at risks beyond the call of duty. Enemy flak takes its toll.

The first 702 pilot to be downed by AA fire over enemy lines was flying close air support when his Skyraider took a hit which starved his engine oil supply. The pilot stuck to the ship and rode it down to a skillful ditch job in a rice paddy. An Air Force helicopter pilot hovering nearby saw his plight, and before he could yell, "Pancake!" the angel was alongside—soon the naval aviator and his Air Force comrade-in-arms were flapping their way back to Seoul—and safety.

Two days later, another pilot of 702 was rescued from a position some 200 miles deep in enemy territory; he was also a victim of enemy flak. He was flying with his division on a bridge buster strike when an enemy AA hit set fire to his plane; things rapidly got so hot that he was forced to hit the silk. While he parachuted down into some scrub pine, his plane dug its own fiery grave on a hillside. The division finished off their job on the target while escorting Corsair fighters buzzed angrily over the downed aviator to discourage would-be enemy snipers. Meanwhile, the pilot climbed painfully to a better protective position. A couple of hours later he was picked up by a helicopter from a Task Force 77 carrier, and whisked back to the *Boxer*—he received prompt medical treatment for his second-degree burns, and lived to fly again. Entitled to an early release from the Navy (he was a volunteer reserve) he is now Mr. "Civilian."

The heavy cruiser U.S.S. *Toledo* has twice played host to one of 702's pilots following similar disagreements with enemy flak near Wonsan. The first time, his division, "Thurston's Raiders," had just finished knocking out three bridges, and was finishing off ammunition by strafing railroad cars—during a run, a flak hit disabled his engine. He elected to bail out and parachuted into a pine grove. Just off Wonsan Bay, the cruiser *Toledo* was pounding shore installations with her heavy guns, so the downed pilot's flight leader radioed the *Toledo* for help. The *Toledo* helicopter was soon on its way, and the naval aviator was aboard the cruiser in time for lunch.

Less than a month later, enemy gunners forced a repeat performance in the same locality. This time, the pilot was able to stay with his plane, making a ditch landing in Wonsan Bay. Again the *Toledo*'s angel was summoned by radio, and flew only a short distance to reach him. He was made an honorary crew member of the *Toledo*, but the captain of the cruiser remarked that the next time he visited his ship, he would be expected to come aboard in a more orthodox manner—via the gangway! Sometimes pilots have had to nurse their planes, badly damaged by flak, to friendly landing strips south of the 38th parallel. Others with less damage have returned to make skillful landings aboard ship in spite of having controls partially shot away. The threat of enemy anti-aircraft fire over Korea is continuous, and growing; more than one pilot has admitted to the feeling of "butterflies" in the stomach before takeoff on such missions.

The Airplanes

Three basic types of aircraft have been flying from the fast carriers of Task Force 77 on missions over Korea. Grumman F9F Panthers are jets, used for fast reconnaissance and fighter cover. Chance Vought F41.1 Corsairs, veterans of the last war, are fighterbombers, known to pilots as "Hawgs." And the superb Douglas AD Skyraiders, attack bombers and workhorses of the fleet, carry the greatest bombload of all three types. Skyraiders are affectionately known as "Able Dawgs." Working together, the "Hawgs" and "Able Dawgs" make up the Navy's efficient close air support and interdiction teams.

Skyraider pilots of 702 show continued amazement at the capabilities of their own planes—that a single-engined plane such as this AD can lift the bombload of a wartime, four-engined B-17 flying fortress from a few hundred feet of carrier deck-run! Once this load has been dropped, the Able Dawg becomes as fast and agile as the best conventional prop-driven fighter. Among all services, the Navy's Able Dawg is recognized as the airplane best suited to the close air support role. These prop-driven planes call carry greater loads and spend more time over the target than can the jets. Should enemy, air opposition enter the close air support picture, then more of our own jets will have to be used for fighter cover. Prop-driven attack bombers, powered by gas turbines, will eventually replace the Skyraider; their development is now being pushed ahead by the Navy. For obsolescence, arch-enemy of all military craft, makes this development vital. The Skyshark, a turbo-prop version of the Skyraider, is a promising result of this development program. Meanwhile, the versatile Skyraider continues to be the most welcome sight to ground forces in Korea when they need close air support.

The Enlisted Men

Without the enlisted men, there could be no planes, no squadron, no air operations. In 702, their manifold skills are devoted to one end: to keep the planes in the air. There are many specialists—hydraulics and engine experts, radio and electronicsmen, parachute riggers, instrumentmen, and metalsmiths. Maintenance is their job. Responsible for all aircraft guns, bombs and armament are the hardworking ordnancemen; they load the guns and hang the heavy bombs. Their tasks are often back-breaking, and are frequently done at night on the unlit carrier decks, no matter what the weather.

Every airplane on the carrier is assigned a man who is its "plane captain." He is with the plane constantly, whenever it is not aloft; ministers to its every need, and helps the pilot in and out of the cockpit with flight gear. He is responsible for making hundreds of "checks" on the plane daily, keeps it fueled and wiped down, maneuvers it into position when it is moved on deck, chocks the wheels and ties the plane down wherever it may end up. Arising before dawn on busy strike days, he puts in many hours, leaving the plane only after it is finally loaded and spotted for the next day's launch. He rests while the plane is over the target—at the same time, he "sweats out" the mission from take-off to recovery—as if plane and pilot were his own personal property.

Side Glances at 702

Men and pilots from other states had enlarged the squadron complement, but the unit still retained its identity as the Dallas squadron. Nearly every original member had a hand in the design of the squadron insigne, which depicts a wiry, charging longhorn steer with smoke puffing from his nostrils. The steer's scraggy tail brandishes a rocket. Bombs and torpedoes are hung from his horns. A large "D" is branded on the steer's hindquarters, and a lone star sets off the design.

Although flying daily strikes over Korea is a deadly serious business, morale is high . . . humor is not absent, and it eases over some of the rougher days. For a time, the squadron lacked a good watchword. There was a great need for a colorful exclamatory statement pilots could use to describe a successful strike—correspondents and public information officers are always looking for an expression with a touch of originality that is suitable for publication. Fictional Navy pilot Crewson's classic of the last war ("There I was, on my back, at 30,000 feet . . .") was outmoded. At last, and quite naturally, an expression was evolved. In truth, there was a lack of originality since the expression was gleaned from some of the more sanguine Air Force releases, but it seemed appropriate from every standpoint. It is now a rare thing to hear pilots, back from a flight, enter the ready room without uttering those hallowed words, "Boy, we clobbered 'em!" Similarly, there is a new appellation for the pilot who really "clobbers 'em". To earn the designation of "tiger," he must have scored many direct hits on a bridge, or must have had outstanding results on his mission. No pilot can be a tiger if he can report nothing but near-misses on a bridge, even if he sarcastically adds, "But the bridge is still shaking!" This is reserved for a bad day, when a strike may not have been too successful, due to flak, weather, or other factors. More often, the first thing the air intelligence officer hears from his interrogation is, "Boy, we were all tigers today!"

One day, one of the 702 pilots was launched in an Able Dawg which developed engine trouble as his division was joining up to head for the target. He radioed for permission to return aboard ship and turned into the landing pattern with his engine power rapidly fading. On the final turn, things became so critical that he lost control and spun into the sea.

The *Boxer*'s angel quickly fished him out of the drink. Unfortunately, the Able Dawg sank quickly and ingloriously. A few days later, a unique ritual took place in 702's ready room. The pilot was awarded a citation unprecedented in the history of Naval Aviation:

The Kremlin
15 May 1951
From: The Commissar—Awards and Decorations
To: The Working Masses of the World
Subj: Assistant Hero of the Soviet Union; awarding of

CITATION

To LT. (now Midshipman) John R. Toughluck USNR, for his outstanding skill, dexterity and intrepid technique in handling an aircraft, the Kremlin, by direct order of that true comrade, hailed by all, our own Uncle Joe, bestows and confers on Lt. (now Midshipman) John R. Toughluck, USNR, the order of Assistant Hero of the Soviet Union; said order to be worn henceforth and forevermore and Lt. (now Midshipman) John R. Toughluck, USNR, shall be entitled to all its rights and privileges from this date forward.

Lt. (now Midshipman) John R. Toughluck, USNR, above and beyond the call of duty, did, in keeping with the highest purging traditions of the Soviet Union, against the inherent stability of the filthy capitalistic Douglas Skyraider aircraft, on 11 May 1951, maneuver said lousy capitalistic aircraft into such a position as to effect total and complete destruction of said degenerate aircraft.

/s/ Ivan Michailovitch
Airman Recruit (1/2 class)
Soviet Air Force

Amid a background of boisterous laughter, the duty officer pompously read the citation, and the pilot accepted with a few words in Russian (he had studied the language in college). A tape recording of the entire proceeding was made by a journalist from the Navy's public information offices in Tokyo. Later the recording was released and broadcast by Armed Forces Radio Service in Tokyo as a part of a Navy program. When the news came back to the *Boxer* that there were some red faces in the Navy public 111 formation office because the Soviet Embassy in Tokyo protested against this "slanderous broadcast, the participants were even more amused!"

Incidentally, that group of "filthy capitalistic" Douglas aircraft which Toughluck started out with that day succeeded knocking out two key railroad bridges. In northwest Korea, cutting vital supply lines to the enemy west sector; another addition to the remarkable record the reserves are setting. Since arriving in the combat zone, every 702 pilot has averaged, in terms of distance flown, more than once around the world at the equator. The total weight of bombs dropped by the *Boxer*'s air group has long since exceeded that expended by any aircraft carrier during World War II.

From the youngest plane captain to the Squadron skipper, the reserves have a common desire; to finish up the job in Korea and get back home. It is fortunate that there are many other trained and ready reserves on tap to join the fight when needed. This very fact may be the blessing that will prevent their being called. Meanwhile, the standby squadrons, part of the team that is the Navy, join the United Nations bulwark against the seas of aggression.

A graduate in mechanical engineering from Rice Institute, **Lieutenant Vernor** was commissioned in the Naval Reserve in 1944. He served in the U.S.S. *Burke* (APD-65) with AmPhibsPac. In 1947–50 he worked as a test engineer with Chance Vought Aircraft, joining the Naval Air Reserve in Dallas, Texas, in 1949. He was called to active duty with reserve squadron VA-702 in 1950, serving as air intelligence officer during their combat tour off Korea, based aboard the U.S.S. *Boxer* (CV-21). He is now an assistant air intelligence officer on the staff of ComAirPac.

11

"The Naval Reserve Should Work"

Captain James G. Abert, USNR

U.S. Naval Institute *Proceedings*
(February 1980): 49–53

THE ONLY CURRENT RATIONALE for reserve forces is training for wartime mobilization. The need for reservists, however, exists not only in their potential wartime service but for peacetime contributory use as well. Sometimes called "mutual support," this second role needs to be addressed separately and not linked, as it is today. Peacetime use is justified now only in terms of its value as mobilization training. However, in most respects, peacetime use is distinctly different from training for wartime, although there is an overlap in that use is often good training. Unfortunately, merging the two concepts, as is done now, leads to less than optimal use of the talent available and creates management difficulties. Today's practice also seriously limits the use of the peacetime work concept for advancing the "worth" of the reserves. In this regard, advancing a dual reserve rationale can open up a second front in the annual contest with the Office of the Secretary of Defense and Congress for scarce defense resources. The basic rationale for maintaining reserve forces rests on economic grounds. If resources were unlimited, then only if the supply of regulars could not meet the demand at any price would one turn to reservists.

The contributory use of reserve assets has been advanced before and without success. Even so, a properly structured peacetime support concept has unassailable economic underpinnings. The "work done" concept may require new legislation. But Congress has been a strong supporter of the Naval Reserve and has not shown itself inflexible to new thoughts as to how to bring about an improved overall defense posture. The idea of dual philosophies does not necessarily imply equality in the number of reservists supported by each rationale, nor equal expenditures, but rather a rough parity in importance in the overall scheme of things.

While much peacetime contributory work is done today, there is no single senior official spokesman within the Navy, reserve or active-duty, responsible only for contributory use. There is no focal point in the management structure which directs subordinates to seek out such opportunities for the Naval Reserve, which inventories the talent available, and which argues for the utilization of reservists in this role. Opportunities are developed and the support given at various management levels simply because it makes good sense to do it. In this respect, it is mainly adhoc and not an organized thrust. If there are exceptions to this, they are principally in the intelligence community.

In the past, the term "contributory support" has been used to attempt to rationalize a potpourri of different types of reserve use, many of which were not cost-effective in that it would have been more efficient to have another full-time regular or to have hired the skills in the civilian marketplace. This is probably one of the reasons peacetime work, apart from training, has had difficulty in gaining general acceptance and adoption as an official program, even though a substantial amount of such work is indeed accomplished.

There is a bit of "Catch-22" associated with present-day contributory efforts. If the Naval Reserve publicizes such contributory support, it could find some of its most useful assets taken out of drill-pay status because the individuals are too well-trained. An argument advanced by those who favor cutting the drilling reserve is that if such persons are that well-trained, they do not need to be paid to get further trained. However, while the drills are not important from a training standpoint, they are important for the opportunity they afford to do contributory work. The idea of mutual support has merit in meeting this argument. Contributory support by reservists can be generalized under two headings:

- Responding to peacetime "peak load" requirements imposed on the active forces
- Providing specialists in blue suits to assist the peacetime active forces in areas in which particular types of knowledge and skills developed by the reservists in their civilian endeavors are needed. In these cases, past Navy experience is seen as materially improving the value of the work product.

Bringing into being a component of the Naval Reserve whose purpose is clearly oriented to fulfilling these needs calls for an explicit management organization. The justification for continuing the personnel involved in this component of the Navy's total force (regular and reserve) is not their need upon mobilization. They would represent a reserve increment beyond the numbers required for mobilization. Indeed, as individuals, they may not have significant mobilization potential because of age and seniority. Instead, retention, pay, and promotion would be based on peacetime contribution to the total force.

Reserve Missions: In recent years, there has been an increased concern with the missions assigned to the Naval Reserve and a demand, particularly on the part of Congress, for a greater degree of integration of active and reserve manpower and missions. A large number of studies have been completed, leading to several reorganizations. The focus has been on "hardening" the requirements for reserves in the event of mobilization. The problem is that forecasting needs for an uncertain future event is a speculative endeavor. Predicting the level and composition of active naval forces is difficult in itself. If the future is cloudy as to the active Navy's requirements, then the task of determining reserve requirements is like trying to hook an anchor to a cloud. This is a weakness of the mobilization rationale. The proposal advanced here would contribute to purposeful integration of reservists and regulars. It is an approach that is not susceptible to the criticism that the future conflict may not be the one anticipated, since peacetime contribution is much nearer and more certain.

Substituting Active-duty for Work for Drills: The proposals advanced here are not meant to lower the absolute level of individual involvement. In fact, for many in the contributory portion of the Naval Reserve, the involvement could be greater. It ought to be possible to pay for the work done and to permit flexibility in the use of the time allocated. It should not be necessary to limit the paid periods to four four-hour segments, principally on weekends. In effect, one would trade drills for larger amounts of what may be called active-duty for work. For example, those reservists who work in command and control for fleet exercises often do not need 48 drills to prepare for a 14-day active-duty stint. If contributory support is the objective, it should allow for the bulk of the funds now expended for these individuals' drills to be reprogrammed to their "active-duty for work" role.

Only a relatively small number of reservists is required for the contributory group. Because most of the contributory-type activities would be tailored to specific active-duty needs, it ought to be possible to find, almost on a case-by-case basis, sufficient personnel to meet what might be unusual time commitments measured against today's requirements. There is at least one Naval Reserve unit that now drills on weekdays during the day. It is a small unit in a relatively large city, and there are always sufficient candidates for the billets. Also, there are many reservists who now put in more than 48 drills and 14 days of active-duty for training. Indeed, it is surprising how many reservists can and will respond with service well beyond the minimum requirements when they have the opportunity to make a useful contribution.

If the proposals advanced here were adopted, it would be to little avail, in terms of the larger purpose, if a flexible management philosophy and a dedication of the necessary resources to carry out the more complex administrative activities did not go hand in hand.

Peacetime Peak Load Uses: The peak load justification for peacetime use of reservists is based on the same principle that keeps civilian temporary manpower agencies in business. The total force would have a reservist only when it needs help beyond that available from active-duty personnel. A recurring example is reserve augmentation of command centers for fleet exercises. The exercises impose peak loads on the regular staffs. Yet, the billets which these individuals occupy during the exercises may have low priority in terms of their relative need upon mobilization. It also may be difficult to defend their need on mobilization day rather than later. This is the reason that staff billets which most reservists rendering these services occupy are among those which the Office of the Secretary of Defense annually suggests dropping from the drill-pay category.

A typical peak load case is that in which reservists are integrated with active-duty personnel as umpires in the portion of the Commander in Chief Atlantic Fleet tactical command readiness program conducted once a quarter at the Naval War College. Over the last two years, on the average, a dozen reservists have been involved in each war game as umpires. The once-a-quarter demand is not sufficient to justify additional staff at the War College. To meet it without the Naval Reserve would require additional duty by individuals from the Atlantic fleet. This use of reservists is thus cost-effective, and there is an additional advantage. Because of personnel shifts among the regulars, it is the reservists who constitute a cadre of umpiring experience in the games. Use of reservists in this role also avoids the adding of yet another requirement to those already levied on the reduced staffs or the overtaxed Atlantic Fleet operating forces. However, there are management problems in deciding whether to develop and stick to a cadre of qualified umpires or to rotate the assignments, because the umpire function is indeed good training. The Atlantic Fleet's view is to stick to the tried, tested, and true; the reserve mobilization training philosophy would call for individuals to rotate. Also a problem is the fact that the billets occupied by the personnel who do the umpiring are in many different offices of the Atlantic Fleet staff. The office that runs the tactical readiness program does not have a mobilization requirement equivalent to the number of umpires needed. According to the current system, all officers whose billets are justified by CinCLantFlt's mobilization requirements should do their 14 days of annual active-duty for training in the offices in which their mobilization billets are located. This is not possible if the war game peak load is to be met.

Another peak load opportunity is on-board ship data collection. This chore is usually imposed on members of the ship's force, and they often have only a vague idea of the whys and wherefores. Sometimes, hard-earned shore duty becomes sea duty again as junior officers are dispatched to sea, in temporary additional duty status, to assist in the data collection effort. Often contractors or civil service personnel are used. There have been recent examples of direct Naval Reserve participation in this type of activity with excellent results. Reservists are demonstrably better and less expensive than civilians on board ship. It is conceivable that Naval Reserve teams could be assembled and placed at the disposal of commands with data collection requirements. There is no need for a set number of drills, and there is no real need to have the individuals aligned with mobilization billets; they would simply be there to do particular jobs, when needed.

Peak load should not be confused with the idea of reservists coming in on back-to-back (or overlapping) 14-day active-duty tours to fill a billet. If the billet needs filling all the time or even 75% of the time, a full-time regular probably is the cost-effective method. Taking into account management costs and travel and per diem, the use of back-to-back reservists is an expensive way to fill a billet. It also incurs very high man-year costs, and even though the retirement component may be less, current costs, as distinct from those that are deferred, are considerably more. It has been said that because reservists have to show their stuff in ten working days, they are quickly off the mark and more productive overall than a single full-year active-duty incumbent. This may be true, but it is a more difficult argument to make than the peak load one, and for this reason is only mentioned and not strongly advocated here.

Inventorying of peak load possibilities is an important aspect of the program. In the main, the key to identification is that the demand be regular and recurring. (Crises can be handled, but they are more difficult.) Scheduled exercises have already been mentioned. The preparation for and the attendance at annual, semiannual, or quarterly meetings such as occur in tactical development and evaluation are particularly amenable to Naval Reserve contributions, since there are a fairly large number of reservists employed in civilian life in weapons test and evaluation. Another area that comes to mind is the preparation of recurring reports. In addition, we might look to temporary staffing deficits caused by sending people to short-term service schools and to the fact that leave requests are more numerous at certain times than at others. Planning for uncovered relief situations might be considered as well.

It is useful to realize that the peak load concept applies to enlisted personnel as well as officers. Suppose, on an experimental basis, that next year roughly 200 enlisted personnel, who had put in their papers for release from active-duty and were headed for college, were specially recruited to replace active-duty individuals who were away from their regular duty stations to attend schools for extended periods. Of course, before becoming reservists, they would have to be recommended for such a program by their active-duty stations. The idea would be to return them to their ships or stations, on schedule, the next summer. Essentially, contracts would be written with the individuals—summer job offers they could rely on. There would be no drills involved during the year, because not enough time would have elapsed for obsolescence to set in. Not having to go to drill could be very desirable to many. They would have another night or weekend free for academics or other aspects of college life for which they would undoubtedly be making some financial sacrifice. Finally, from a straight financial standpoint, it would probably be more rewarding than any other summer employment they might obtain.

Specialist in a Blue Suit: Contributory support provides an opportunity for the Navy to "hire" Naval Reservists on the basis of specialized civilian skills. Examples are computer systems analysts, engineers, educational specialists, and personnel managers. In many cases, from a pure cost standpoint, blue stirs, compensation is often less than the rate for the service in the marketplace where the regular Navy would otherwise have to purchase it.

A number of objections can be raised: unfair competition, conflict of interest, possible misuse of appropriated funds, and perhaps others. To be sure these dangers exist. But because they exist does not mean they cannot be handled. First, the program should be specifically and openly managed. Second, the program should be limited in size by policy determination. For example, an appropriation could be earmarked explicitly for this purpose which would set a ceiling on the amount of such support provided. The conflict-of-interest issue is more difficult. The control of conflict of interest would rely mainly on good judgment. Clearly, occasions for direct conflict should not be allowed.

Using these specially qualified reservists should not be done simply for cost-saving considerations, even as in a total force concept. The special reason for log an ex-blue suiter, rather than a contractor, must be that there is a particular advantage to receiving the advice from one who has a Navy background and essentially directs his main loyalty, while he is in his blue suit, to the Navy. He may be a contractor himself, but it is asserted that putting on the blue suit takes the edge off the usual contractor marketing instinct. Note also should be taken of the fact that in terms of an advisory role, even though he has donned military attire, the reservist is not totally beholden to the active Navy chain of command. Even though he will receive a fitness report, it is only one of many from numerous commands as far as promotion is concerned, and Navy pay is not his sole means of economic support. The point is, he may be more critical and offer counter views where regular Navy staff members know, or at least feel they know, what is policy, or often, what the admiral wants.

It is important to remember that the reserve specialist comes to the problem with a Navy background. Most readers are familiar with the solutions often advanced by "outside" experts with no Navy experience—a preponderance of theory, but little practical experience to temper it. Ironically, the capabilities of these blue-suit specialists would not be there had the individuals stayed 365-day regulars, since their skills are based mainly on their civilian expertise. Note also that drills for training are not necessary to justify either the concept or the individual's retention in the Naval Reserve.

Frequently, very talented persons in the naval warfare and management areas join the reserve. Often their civilian positions are well above their positions the Navy hierarchy. Nevertheless, it is possible to make these persons available in their blue suits as consultants and advisors, and perhaps as sounding boards, to senior naval officers. In effect, they could serve as a check on staff. And the effect would be better by drawing from the reserve talent pool rather than recruiting by chance encounter or otherwise—often based on the "old boy network" or "school tie" is now the case.

At present there is no inventory of reservist skills maintained for the specialist purpose. Nor is there any explicit allocation of resources to pay for this use talent. Perhaps it should be charged to the active Navy budget rather than the Naval Reserve budget. This would make sense from a resource allocation standpoint. When it happens now, it is free to the user. Details and organizational forms for this can be worked out later, because it is essentially a matter of shifting budgets and a realignment in terms of who is charged with their justification.

Paying for Work: Use of the plan suggested here would inevitably involve a competition for budgetary resources, both within the Naval Reserve and between regulars and reservists. Unless value is truly given, the Naval Reserve clearly will not fare well. Some may question whether the comparison between reservist and regular can or will be fairly made, and this concern should not be dismissed lightly. Nevertheless, it is a matter beyond the scope of this article, which attempts only to develop and argue the rationale for a second, or dual, reserve perspective.

Paying for the work—not the training—is a "new" premise. Today's management systems are set up to reward the achievement of the training objective and to penalize and make difficult any straying from this path. Significant actions will be necessary to organize and manage the thrust advanced here.

Summary: There are now many examples of reservists already effectively doing what is advocated here—stretching peacetime resources. The idea is to do it explicitly. Contributory support has been advanced in the past, but it has not been sold. Selling means clearly defining what the product is and what it is not. It means justifying it on its own merits and not as an adjunct which is virtually subservient to mobilization training. If sold in concept, the question then becomes "How much?" In this regard, having a second rationale should set up forces which produce not only better resources allocation within the Naval Reserve, but indeed between the active and reserve components of the Navy's total force.

Captain Abert recently completed a tour as commanding officer of CinCLantFlt detachment 206, Washington, D.C., a reserve unit which supports various staff elements of the Commander in Chief Atlantic Fleet. In civilian life he is vice president for research and development of the National Center for Resource Recovery. He is a former Deputy Assistant Secretary for Program Evaluation at HEW. His active naval career (1954–1960) included service in the USS *Midway* (CVA-41), USS *Boston* (CAG-1), USS Hugh *Purvis* (DD-709), USS *Sabalo* (SS-302), and the NROTC unit at the University of North Carolina: He holds a Ph.D. in economics (1966) from Duke University and a B.S. in mechanical engineering (1954) from the University of South Carolina.

12 "The Reserve's Biggest Problem"

Vice Admiral Robert F. Dunn, USN

U.S. Naval Institute *Proceedings*
(October 1984): 66–72

TODAY'S NAVAL RESERVE is on the move—"in renaissance," says the Chief of Naval Operations. Its missions are expanding; its numbers are growing; its equipment is modernizing and filling out. Today, reserves are at sea, in the air, and ashore. They train with the active forces. They do training of the active forces. They augment the active forces. They are ready to perform missions for which the active forces are not trained. They preserve the talent of the active forces. They perform special studies and analyses, sit on selection boards, represent the Navy in the civilian world, and represent the civilian world to the Navy. They do more than the active Navy realizes. They do more than Congress appreciates. They do a lot. But the Naval Reserve has the capacity to do more.

Despite today's unprecedented operational tempo, the Navy does not need as large a force structure in peacetime as it would in war. To maintain an unnecessarily large Navy in peacetime would waste tax dollars. To maintain active force capabilities and skills needed only in full-scale war is also a waste. Yet, in modern war, there will be little time to train and equip all the people, ships, aircraft squadrons, construction battalions (SeaBees), medical teams, and other specialized units needed.

A strong, well-trained, well-equipped, and well-organized Naval Reserve enables us to have just such a posture: active forces to meet peacetime commitments and crises; active and reserve forces to meet the requirements of war.

Regrettably, the Navy is only partially structured to enable the Naval Reserve to take on a larger load. For years, we have attempted to build the Navy to meet every commitment and every war plan with forces in being assigned only to the active Navy. Only when faced with a budgetary or political constraint have we turned to the reserve for help, frequently with seeming reluctance. Thus, we have developed a force structure of ships and air squadrons—some with reserve augment units, some without—largely dependent upon whether or not the Office of the Chief of Naval Operations (OpNav) sponsor can afford to "buy out" all the billets. Commissioned Naval Reserve Force (NRF) ships and aircraft squadrons are in the Navy force structure because there happens to be equipment and people available. For similar budget and political reasons, we have placed all of our domestic organic airlift and all of our combat search and rescue helicopter forces in the Naval Reserve with no capability for surging to meet crises other than that provided by limited numbers of assigned full-time personnel or reserve volunteers. Other examples of random reserve assignment to mission abound. But there remains no science to the methodology for determining optimum active/reserve force mix. Instead, it has pretty much all "just happened."

The Naval Reserve has almost always grown in tune with the historical reserve mission of training for mobilization. A more recent impetus to growth has been a demand for reserve forces to take over peacetime missions to reduce active personnel end strength. Within limits, this can be done, but these limits must be defined. Active/reserve mixes in individual deployable units can be adjusted, but there will be peacetime capability problems if the active Navy is excessively reduced in either numbers or particular skills. Active/reserve mixes among units can capitalize on reserve potential and generally lessen cost, but at the expense of increasing operational tempo for deployable active ships and, perhaps, reducing the numbers of ships available for forward deployments. Whole missions might be given over to the reserve force, but contingencies short of presidential call-up must be planned. For example, Naval Control of Shipping is assigned to the Naval Reserve with little risk of being caught short in a crisis without call-up. On the other hand, the minesweeping mission is well within the capabilities of the reserve, but the active forces must retain some minimum capacity to sweep to preclude lack of capability should a vital passage be mined when reserve call-up is not possible. One reason the active/reserve force mix is not better defined is because for years, reserve issues have been clouded in a milieu of myth. Although there has been no shortage of emotion, polemics, and politics, virtually widespread understanding of the Naval Reserve exists.

The most prevalent myth about the Naval Reserve is that it has little to offer in the way of personnel talent. Reservists are too often perceived as a group of non-producers who could not stand the rigors of active Navy life, or as freeloaders, or both. Nothing could be further from the truth. The typical reservist is a patriot. Many are prior-service veterans who have elected to pursue a different career pattern than their active-duty contemporaries. They are no less dedicated, no less skillful, and no less officers or sailors. The vast majority are true volunteers. They give up their weekends and, very often, much other time as well in order to drill. They often forego vacations to perform annual active duty for training (AcDuTra). They frequently risk the displeasure of their full-time employers for spending so much time on Navy business. They and their families are Navy through and through. Reservists form an experienced resource anxious and willing to put their skills to work in preparing the Navy to be ready to fight and win at sea.

A second myth about the reserve is that even if trained and organized, its members will not rally to the colors when called. Most often, this charge is made in connection with an apocryphal tale about how the air reserves could or would not get ready for combat during the 1968 Pueblo Crisis call-up. The story comes replete with descriptions of aviators turning in their wings and enlisted people trying to opt out in other ways. The fact is the squadrons did report. Attitudinally, most were ready to go. A few individuals did quit, but it was actually active Navy that let down the majority of reservists who were ready by not providing them modern aircraft with up-to-date service changes, support equipment, spares, and other necessities to turn them into combat ready outfits.

Ignored by many when telling this story are the numbers of Navy pilots who found ways to steer clear of combat while continuing on active duty. Ignored are the numbers of Navy enlisted people who found ways to avoid Southeast Asian cruises. Ignored is the story of the well-organized and will-led reserve SeaBees who wrote such a successful chapter in their history during the Vietnam War. Ignored, too, are the stories of the thousands of individual reservists—aviation, surface, intelligence, medical, and supply officer and enlisted personnel—who volunteered for active service during the Vietnam War. Reservists will report when called. Many will volunteer before they are called. They may not be full-time officers and sailors, but they are dedicated officers and sailors ready at moment's notice to report for duty. All they request is the mission and the training.

If reserves are going to be ready for mobilization or ready to contribute to any other sort of active duty, they must be trained. The major responsibility for this training should be the active Navy's. But for a number of reasons, the priorities of current operations principal among them, reserve training has too often been shunted to others. Most often, it is pushed on the reserves themselves or to those full-time active-duty reservists assigned to training and administration of reserves—the TARs—another community swathed in myth. The TAR community, or a community very similar to it in function, is necessary to a well-organized, well-trained, and ready-to-operate Naval Reserve. The reserves of every service have some full-time personnel assigned to provide training, continuity of effort, and administration. If the Navy did not have TARs, it would have to assign regulars to do the job. The Marine Corps, the Coast Guard, and Navy SeaBees do that now. But it is expensive in terms of active personnel end strength, and it is not, regrettably, a career-enhancing assignment. There have been proposals to replace officer TARs with regulars, but such proposals have come to naught. Meanwhile, the TARs do the job and do it well, in spite of the myths that surround their program.

TARs are almost universally saddled with a bad image. Regulars look askance; reserves do not trust them; and the TARs themselves are paranoid toward any non-TAR who questions their way of doing business. But these generalized images are false. TARs fall along the normal distribution curves of dedication and performance like members of any other community. The problem is that for too long, they have worked outside the mainstream of the active Navy. Consequently, they are unknown to much of the active Navy and suspected by the reserves for perceived lack of recent operational experience. Coupled with the need to administer precisely an over-bureaucratized reserve system, misunderstandings are created. The cure is to de-bureaucratize the reserve system and to get the TARs into the fleet.

Only a few TARs do get to the fleet on regular assignment because of the lack of push by the active forces for them to do so. This situation has its roots in the TAR mythology and is perpetuated by inertia inherent in those who have been ashore for too long. In the officer ranks, the problem is intensified by the active Navy perception that TAR officers at sea take up billets needed for career progression by regular officers. Then, too, addition of sea duty requirements for TARs beyond those currently existing in NRF ships and squadrons adds significant numbers to TAR inventory requirements. This is an expensive adjustment. Finally, in earlier years, TARs were recruited to the program with the implication that they would seldom go to sea. Some who were recruited under those conditions are still serving.

The TAR community is changing, however. Quality cuts for accession are high. Only top performers need apply, and they are told to expect sea duty. The TAR is becoming more like the regular member. The only difference is that his or her subspecialty is reserve management. It bodes well for the TARs, the Naval Reserve, and the whole Navy.

As good as the TARs may become and as dedicated as the reservists may be, together they can only provide to a limited extent the focus needed for a genuinely contributing reserve program. The real focus must come from the active Navy. First, the active Navy must define the mission, the skills, and the numbers required of the reserve. Once that is accomplished, the active Navy gaining commands must play their part.

The gaining command is the active Navy organization to which a reserve unit will report upon mobilization. In the case of commissioned reserve units—those units that have their own equipment, such as ships, air squadrons, SeaBees, and cargo-handling battalions—the gaining command will often be a fleet commander in chief or some other operational commander. In the case of augmenting units—those units generally composed of trained people without equipment who will bring active unit manning up to that required at mobilization day—the gaining commands are individual ships, squadrons, stations, all, staffs. To realize the potential payoff in terms of first-class training for both the active and reserve forces, the gaming command must play its part with dedication and vigor.

Each active Navy unit must know what its own reserve unit is doing to provide for mobilization training, guide that training, manage that training, and make it meaningful in terms of mission. The gaining command must use its reserve component at every opportunity. It must insist on performance, maintain communications, and demand that unit drills, weekend away training (WET), and AcDuTra be performed at the gaining command whenever possible. Also, whenever possible, key personnel from the gaining command should visit the unit's home base. This involvement is crucial to both the reserve unit and to what value the reserve unit may be to the gaining command in peace-time. The attitude of a disinterested gaining command cannot be overcome by the most dedicated reserve unit. Conversely, an interested and involved gaining command results in an outstanding reserve unit.

Those gaining commands that do make maximum use of the efforts and talents of their reserve units often have the best-trained and most ready units. The active and reserve personnel consider themselves partners in readying themselves for the unit's mission. Active-duty personnel provide the leadership and the up-to-date skills in tactics, maintenance, and administration. Reservists provide experience, talent, and supplementary manpower. Active-duty personnel are busy readying for deployment, on deployment, planning for maintenance or overhaul, or are in maintenance or overhaul. Often, they cannot part from the task at hand long enough to plan ahead. Reservists can help. In some units, there is insufficient active-duty manpower to do the job. Reservists can help. In special projects, studies, temporary manpower support, exercise planning, and myriad other ways, reservists can help. What they have done in recent months in personnel augment during crises, airlift, intelligence, and planning is legion. What they can do in the future is limited only by dollars, time, and the imagination of the active Navy.

Although the gaining command is key to the success of its own reserve unit, it cannot by itself guarantee that success. Most certainly, the reserves and the full-time active-duty people in the unit play critical roles. But it also takes dedicated effort on the part of the reserve organization and the reserve program sponsor are second only to those of the gaining command in ensuring the success of the Naval Reserve programs.

Each reserve unit, whether designated as a commissioned or augmenting unit, falls within the purview of a specified OpNav program sponsor. This sponsor is either a deputy chief of naval operations or a director of a major staff office. The program sponsor is charged with supporting his assigned reserve programs with billets, dollars, and equipment. Because there was cloudy and often contradictory guidance given to the sponsors for so many years, the various reserve programs had checkered support. In the absence of clear active/reserve force mix guidance, sponsors would allocate only a minimum of the scarce resources to the reserve programs. Poorly structured, poorly manned, and poorly equipped reserve units resulted. In some cases, only the various reserve lobbies and Congress kept the programs going.

Having observed the successes of such programs as Intelligence, Sea-Bees, and several facets of aviation, former Chief of Naval Operations Admiral Thomas B. Hayward, his successor, Admiral James D. Watkins, and Secretary of the Navy John Lehman realized that the quality of reserve programs hinged on their program sponsors. Consequently, these leaders encouraged program sponsors to attend to their programs. For the first time in years, almost all reserve programs received the attention they deserved, and almost all benefitted from this attention.

Lack of proper equipment with which to train and lack of modern equipment with which to mobilize has been a nagging, frustrating, and seemingly insurmountable problem within the Naval Reserve. Only recently has the Navy realized that lack of modern equipment for the reserve is an active Navy problem as well. If the reserve forces are to be trained and ready for peacetime augmentation, for crisis call-up, or for wartime mobilization, they must train with the equipment with which they must fight. Training on World War II–vintage mockups in a drill hall does not prepare one for steaming a fast frigate. Flying a photo config-ured Crusader does not prepare one for flying an F-14 Tomcat. Working on antiquated gear does not prepare one for the modern Navy. Fortu-nately, Admiral Watkins's "renaissance" is real. Air reserves are flying and working on A-7Es, F-14s, P-3Cs, and F/A-18s. Surface reserves are moving into *Knox*- and *Oliver Hazard Perry*-class frigates. More and more, reservists are training on the equipment with which they will fight. As a result, the Naval Reserve is becoming parallel with the Navy.

Once properly trained on parallel equipment, the reserves can finally make major contributions to the active Navy, and they will, in fact, be ready for call-up, mobilization, and peacetime assistance. Even now, reserves are steaming in frigates on operational missions, flying on operational antisubmarine warfare and drug interdiction missions, and participating in Navy efforts ranging from intelligence support to construction, to medical and legal services, to public affairs and more. In fact, with adequate resources, informed and interested gaining commands, and good mission definition, the Naval Reserve's only limit appears to be in attaining adequate numbers of personnel. The problem soon becomes one of recruiting.

Reserve officers are recruited almost entirely from those officers recently released from active duty. There are a few direct procurement programs in intelligence, law, medical, and other designators, but most officers have had recent sea experience. A designated surface warfare officer or naval aviator is most common. Reserve pay billets are sought after and hard to come by. For this reason, the Chief of Naval Reserve can be selective. Active-duty performance counts, and only the best officers are chosen. This is particularly so in the air community.

The Chief of Naval Reserve seeks his reserve enlisted prospects largely from among the prior-service population. The recruiters have done well in this market in recent years, but all indications point to trouble ahead. Growing reserve requirements coupled with increased active force retention are rapidly drying up the available pool. Those ratings and special skills in short supply in the active Navy are the ratings in short supply in the reserve. Special incentives can help, but even these cannot attract a skill that does not exist. As a result, the Naval Reserve has recently commenced a grow-your-own program.

The reserve organization has always had a limited enlisted grow-your-own program called Ready Mariner. About 2,000 recruiters a year join the reserves for recruit training followed by "A" School, then they spend the balance of a six-year contract in the drilling reserve. As of 1 October 1983, that program was changed in a number of ways, redesignated the Sea and Air Mariner (SAM) program, and increased its goal to 10,000 recruits per year. Not all SAMs will have "A" School seats available; thus a variety of other training stratagems have been devised, all aimed at assuaging the serious skill shortages facing the reserve. The program also attempts to attract young people into the Naval Reserve who want to be in the Navy but cannot leave their home areas for long periods in peacetime because of school, work, or family commitments. One advantage of the SAM program is that recruiting can be better focused on the area in which the Navy needs reservists.

The geographic distribution of reservists, especially enlisted personnel, is a key element in reserve programs. Ideally, a reservist should never have to travel more than 50 miles to his drill site, and his drill site should be his gaining command. This is most important in the case of commissioned units. Unfortunately, this ideal is difficult to attain, considering the numbers of personnel needed to man the growing reserve. Consequently, the 50 miles is stretched to 100 and then even further when airlift can be reasonably assured. As these limits are stretched, cost becomes prohibitive, both to the individual and to the Navy. These demographics not only constrain recruiting but also influence the locating of reserve units and the attainability of the requisite numbers of reservists to do the job. Attainability, in turn, ultimately dictates the achievable mix of reserve manpower in the active/reserve equations.

The Navy is only now beginning to undertake seriously the long overdue analytical search for the optimum active reserve force mix. As it does so, the issues discussed here must be addressed, as must be other important issues. For example, personnel procurement, training, and career progression plans should combine strategies for both the active and reserve forces, near and long term. The economic trade-offs between locating reserve units inland versus providing air transportation to the fleet sites must be made. Further integration of active and reserve crews in elected units and dedicated peacetime missions for the Naval Reserve should be studied. Further involvement of reserve officers in the management of the Naval Reserve must be examined. The possibilities are numerous; the task is immense.

Whatever the result of the active/reserve mix, recruiting, training, gaining command involvement, and program sponsor performance are key factors in producing a strong, ready, and contributing Naval Reserve. But the primary factor is the strong and pervading presence and interest of the active Navy. This interest must start at the top of the uniformed Navy with the Chief of Naval Operations. To keep it tied to the active Navy, it must include an active Navy flag officer as Chief of Naval Reserve. It must include vigorous and enthusiastic active Navy gaining commands. It must include large numbers of active Navy people interested in and involved with the reserves an every level of command. Only then can we achieve an efficient and economical combined force of actives and reserves, working together and reinforcing one another in peace, and ready to fight and win at sea in war.

Vice Admiral Dunn, a 1951 graduate of the U.S. Naval Academy, flew A-1 Skyraiders and A-4 Skyhawks and commanded Attack Squadron 146 while flying combat missions during the Vietnam War. He has also commanded an attack carrier air wing, the USS *Mount Whitney* (LCC-20), USS *Saratoga* (CV-60), the Naval Safety Center, Carrier Group Eight, and the Naval Military Personnel Command. Vice Admiral Dunn served as Chief of Naval Reserve prior to his current assignment as Commander Naval Air Force, U.S. Atlantic Fleet.

"Why Not One Navy"

13

Captain Harlan B. Miller, USNR (Ret.)

U.S. Naval Institute *Proceedings*
(October 1990): 71–77

TODAY'S NAVAL RESERVE has much reason to be proud. Certainly, the Naval Reserve from which I retired in 1986 was far more effective, efficient, and rationally organized than the Reserve I joined in 1962, when I left the regular Navy. But a number of serious problems impair the Reserve's effectiveness, depress reservists' morale, and dramatically limit the Reserve's value as a resource for the active-duty Navy.

Some of the Reserve's problems are exaggerated forms of similar problems in the active-duty Navy. High rates of personnel turnover ensure that one is always behind in training. The need to play catch-up in training also contributes to a paperwork blizzard. The administrative over-head of a typical Reserve unit is immense. A year's worth of fitness reports, evaluations, inspections, medical examinations, advancement examinations, general military training, physical fitness testing, monthly, quarterly, and annual reports, and so on, must be compressed into 24 working days. Unsurprisingly, reservists have to do a lot of the work at home, and "gundecking" is not unheard of. To parody an old Reserve recruiting slogan ("What was good in the Navy is great in the Naval Reserve"), one might say that what's bad in the Navy is worse in the Naval Reserve.

One of the causes of personnel turnover is excessive seniority. This is also a problem in the active-duty Navy, especially among the officers, where it is politely called grade creep. I was once a member of a large Reserve unit with 25 officer billets. All were filled. There were 3 commanders, including the commanding and executive officers, 2 lieutenants, 1 lieutenant (junior grade), and 20 lieutenant commanders.

It is interesting to compare the administrative solutions to the Reserve problem of excessive seniority and the less serious active-duty problem of grade creep. There always seems to be room, perhaps with some gnashing of teeth, in Washington or someplace else ashore for another commander or captain. But in the Reserve the solution is much simpler. One who is promoted in the Naval Reserve, often to lieutenant commander, and almost always to commander or captain, is effectively told, "Congratulations, you're fired." Perversely, it is better to be passed over the first time up for promotion. One failure of selection generally does not endanger an officer's pay billet.

Members of other Reserve components often express astonishment when they encounter the Naval Reserve's nonpay drillers and nonpay units. The threat of nonpay hangs over every officer of the rank of lieutenant or above, depressing morale and sometimes encouraging inappropriate maneuvers to ingratiate oneself with the billet-assigning powers that be. Many, perhaps the most rational, just quit. Others hang on for years in nonpay.

Reserve Centers typically have at least one Volunteer Training Unit (VTU) to which are assigned reservists for whom no pay billet can be found. At large drilling sites, such as the Naval Air Reserve commands at air stations, the VTUs are often "elephant graveyards" where sizable herds of the many-striped wait out their days, some of them with hope of a future pay billet. VTUs often provide important services to pay units, but they are inherently dreary and depressing organizations lacking any real missions. A long-term Naval Reserve officer can avoid serving in nonpay only by miraculous luck or astounding connections. (I spent something more than seven years in nonpay drill status, once for a three-year stretch, and I was more fortunate than many others.)

As the survivors become more and more senior, their value to the active-duty forces decreases. Eventually one is senior to most ship commanding officers and cannot reasonably go to sea except on a large staff. But most staffs and ships and shore commands do not really need more captains and commanders. They could use a good lieutenant or two. Senior reservists are generally treated politely and assigned some type of study that will keep them from getting underfoot.

The statute that ties together regular Navy and Naval Reserve promotion zones by means of the running-mate system also makes the boundary between the active and reserve forces a semipermeable membrane for individual officers. For example:

Two officers, A and B, are commissioned on the same date, and promoted together to lieutenant (junior grade). Two years later, A decides to leave active duty. He resigns from the regular Navy, is commissioned in the Naval Reserve with the same date of rank, is released, and affiliates with the Ready Reserves. He continues to drill and perform annual active duty for training (AT) as he progresses in, let us suppose, the world of banking. But six years later, even though he has become a junior vice president, A concludes that nothing else is as satisfying as naval operations. A, now a lieutenant commander, would like to get back in the regular Navy. But, for all practical purposes, he cannot. Officially, A and B are still peers, perhaps even legal running mates. But for six years B has been in the fleet, or on joint assignments, or whatever, and A has been on active duty a total of no more than 84 days, with another 144 days spent in a Reserve Center. A is now only slightly more competitive with B in the fleet than B would be with A at the bank. You can go out, but you can't come back.

This is not just a problem for A and hundreds like him. It marks substantial institutional inflexibility. The Navy cannot transfer personnel resources from one category to another and back again as needed. It is just not possible to move significant capabilities to a lower level of readiness and have complete confidence in their availability later. The hardware may keep, but the people will not. The Navy's budget will be cut in the next few years. Strengths that cannot somehow be retained in the Reserve must either be bought at full price or lost completely.

We cannot retain strengths in the Reserve unless we get the right people into the right billets. This is never an easy job, and the unit/Reserve Center system makes it nearly impossible. Individual reservists with active-duty experience are scattered across the country by considerations of family, job, education, and so on—which the Navy cannot control, or even influence. Reserve units are assigned to centers in particular locations in accordance with the (estimated) number of potential drilling reservists. But no center could possibly have units with billets for every rank and rate being released from active duty. Further, many sizable towns do not have Naval Reserve Centers.

Therefore, many newly released service members never affiliate with the Reserve in a drilling status. Many that do find that there are no billets in their specialties at any reasonably accessible Reserve Center. At present men and women with skills badly needed in units in Omaha mark time in Atlanta drinking coffee, watching films, and finally leaving in disgust. Others travel great distances for assignments. Some of these travelers, in the Naval Air Reserve and associated programs, are provided with government transportation, which is notoriously unreliable. Others travel at their own expense, sometimes great distances. I drove a bit more than 600 miles round-trip every month for three years to drill in nonpay. That is not a record either for distance or for duration of travel for a nonpay driller. Still, it is too much to ask.

Even when a Naval Reserve unit is fully manned with competent personnel of the appropriate grades, each assigned a significant mobilization billet at the gaining command, the present system imposes great costs. The effort of maintaining the organizational structure of the unit and the higher echelons of command absorb substantial quantities of time and attention.

It is time to ask a deeper question. We are probably administering Naval Reserve units about as efficiently as possible given the current organizational framework. Should we be doing it at all?

Toward Solutions

Why is officer promotion in the Naval Reserve so unlike officer promotion in, say, the Army Reserve? The answer is quite simple. By law Naval Reserve officers are assigned regular Navy running mates and become eligible for promotion at the same time as these running mates.

I have never understood the rationale for this arrangement. For some of the affected reservists it produces the pleasures and (limited) perquisites of high rank. When retirement pay finally begins at age 60 it will be at a high pay grade. The up-or-out system forces others out when they twice fail selection. Both those promoted and those not promoted must leave the jobs they have mastered and may well have enjoyed.

But it is not clear that even the "winners" in the present system are as well off financially and psychologically as those who play the different game in the other services. Recently, I renewed the acquaintance of a high school classmate. He joined the National Guard while in college. When we met again I had just retired from the Ready Reserve rather than serve in a make-work nonpay billet with little prospect of future assignment. He, in contrast, was serving in a pay billet as he had been for more than 30 years. Further, he had every prospect of continuing in such a billet until retirement at age 60. He had not the slightest doubt that he knew his job as well as any active duty officer in the same specialty. His pay grade is W-4, mine the more exalted O-6. But his total remuneration and monthly retirement pay will be higher than mine. Quite likely, the difference is entirely proper—over the years, he has probably contributed more to the nation's military readiness.

Let us set aside the question of pay. (We should be able to do this if we can assume, as does the Navy's policy concerning paying reservists, that it is not deeply insulting to be expected to work for nothing.) There are certainly rewards for those of us who "succeeded" under the present system. We have caps with braid on the brim, better parking spaces at the exchange, sometimes better rooms in the bachelor officers' quarters, and impressive abbreviations under our signatures. But it is not at all obvious that these goodies compare to the deep satisfaction of knowing one's job and knowing that one knows it.

The present promotion system for Naval Reserve officers impedes readiness, shortchanges individuals, and helps no one but the insignia manufacturers. We must change it, but just how we should change it is not clear. Perhaps promotions should be limited to the numbers actually needed to fill billets. Or perhaps some formula could be used to convert Reserve time to equivalent active-duty time. Suppose that for each year in the Naval Reserve one's equivalent time in grade were extended by six months. Selecting the right method will require careful study of the alternatives and of their effects on individuals and on the relation of active and Reserve components.

One of the relevant factors is the need to make the semipermeable membrane between the Naval Reserve and the regular Navy fully permeable. We need a system in which individuals can move more freely from active to Reserve status and back again. Slowing and readjusting the Naval Reserve promotion escalator will achieve part of this goal. In addition, individual reservists must be able to learn, practice, and maintain the skills they need in active-duty billets. They must not be occupied by the maintenance of unnecessary organizational structures.

Further, we need to repeal the legal requirement that one serve the last eight years in the Naval Reserve in order to be eligible for Reserve retirement. In fact, it would make better sense to adopt a version of the present Reserve retirement formula for everyone. A system based on days of active duty plus the various points collected while in a Reserve status would both reduce overall cost to the government and increase the rewards of those who served long periods of active duty.

Let service members, active or Reserve, become eligible for retirement pay when they have collected time on active duty plus Reserve points equivalent to 20 years active duty, or reach age 60, whichever comes first. The costs in higher retirement stipends for some would easily be covered by the savings in training resulting from lower turnover.

Both a cause and an effect of decreasing the training load and the promotion-driven turnover would be keeping reservists in billets long enough for them to learn their jobs.

Accompanying these changes in personnel policies should be a series of organizational changes, which would sharply reduce the time, money, and structure dedicated to the Naval Reserve as an organization.

First, we should abolish all Reserve units that do not mobilize as commands. We should avoid as much as possible the costs in money, time, and attention of administering organizations that would form no part of our order of battle. For example, we should retain the construction battalions, patrol squadrons, small boat units, and mobile mine assembly groups, which would mobilize and serve as units. But we should abolish augmentation units and assign individuals directly to the gaining command. We should scrap units that neither augment nor mobilize, unless some special case can be made for them. The Readiness unit program has provided some valuable steps in this direction; it has sharply decreased the numbers of reservists who must dedicate large parts of their time to unit administration. But we can and should go much further.

If we assign individual reservists directly to commands they need not drill at all. Such reservists would be authorized to perform at least four weeks of AT per year at the command to which they are attached or at appropriate schools. A carrier simply would be assigned a number of personnel who are in Reserve status. For such reservists the Naval Reserve would not be an organization intervening between them and their ship— but rather a supporting organization providing ombudsman services when needed and perhaps backup "ticket-punching" services at Reserve Centers for such matters as physical examinations and general military training when they had missed them on active duty. After years of resistance the Naval Reserve is finally making limited use of the category of

Individual Ready Reserve (IRR), which assigns individuals directly to gaining commands. IRR status should be much more common, with both funding and requirements for increased but flexible AT.

We should be able to reduce the number of drilling units and the number of Reserve Centers. In fact, we might not need any drilling Reserve units at all. For the model I am proposing the difference between an active ship or squadron and a Reserve ship or squadron is that the active command has a large number of active-duty personnel and relatively few Reserve personnel and the Reserve command has the reverse. If we abandon drills and operate our Reserve commands with a mixture of assigned active-duty personnel and those on active duty for training they would be distinguished from other commands only by a lower level and a more uneven tempo of operations. A ship in Reserve status might be assigned 20% of its complement in active-duty personnel and 160% to 320% (or more) in Reserve personnel. In the event of general mobilization, personnel beyond requirements would be assigned to newly built, acquired, or reactivated ships. In normal times coordinated periods of AT would provide adequate manning for substantial scheduled operations.

With this arrangement one need not choose between two extreme states of readiness, one very high and expensive, the other much lower. The Navy could maintain ships or squadrons at intermediate levels with varying mixes of active/Reserve manning. This kind of flexibility could provide attractive alternatives to decreasing real operating budgets.

If we assign individuals directly to gaining commands, without being tied to a Reserve unit and a Reserve Center, we can make the assignments on the basis of skills and needs, not the accidents of geography. This move alone would enormously increase the Naval Reserve's contribution to readiness, as well as ameliorating misassignment and travel problems. Traveling to AT twice a year (and getting paid for it) is much less onerous than traveling to drills every month (and not getting paid for it).

I have compared the Naval Reserve unfavorably to other Reserve components of the armed forces. Navies are unlike armies and air forces in that their primary hardware does not lend itself to distribution about the country. We can have infantry battalions in Kansas and fighter squadrons in Ohio, but destroyer divisions and amphibious groups cannot be homeported in Colorado or West Virginia. But we can profitably learn from the experience of the National Guard and the other Reserves. We are different, and we can be better.

Why is the organizational paradigm for our Reserve Components centered around the drill? My half-informed speculation is that the drill was imprinted on the Reserves at birth, like mother on a just-hatched gosling. The local militia drilled, and it is from the militia that our present Reserve organizations were born. But the local militia was local both in composition and in responsibilities, mobilized as a unit, and served significant social and political purposes as well as military ones. The Naval Reserve's purposes do not at all correspond to those of the old county militia.

Perhaps the weekend militia drill is still a good model for the National Guard, which has some significant similarities to the old militia. But it is not, and probably never has been, the proper model for the Naval Reserve.

It is time to dump the drill. In fact, it is time to dump the Naval Reserve. We should do away with "the Reserve" and make "Reserve" a status, not an organization. We can be one Navy, a better, stronger, happier, yet smaller and cheaper Navy.

Captain Miller currently teaches philosophy at Virginia Polytechnic Institute and State University. He was commissioned through the NROTC program at the University of Virginia. After three years in the Pacific Fleet amphibious force he left active duty and earned AM and PhD degrees. He served 12 tours of varying length in nine different Reserve units and commanded Fleet Intelligence Training Center Atlantic Unit 0107 and Defense Intelligence Headquarters Unit 0307.

14 "The Selected Reserve: The Peace Dividend"

Robert D. Helsel

U.S. Naval Institute *Proceedings*
(October 1990): 74–75

THE NAVY of the 1990s cannot operate on a business as usual philosophy. To meet national and budget requirements, it must reduce overhead expenses and increase productivity. With fewer bodies, the Navy will need the Selected Reserve (SELRES) to support normal as well as crisis situations. The watchwords for SELRES in the 1990s and beyond must include routine augmentation of active forces as well as mobilization readiness.

To answer the call, the Reserve must focus its personnel on peacetime as well as wartime active-duty functions. I propose the following changes.

Organization

Integrated Command: Get rid of the separate-but-equal unit structure. Under the one-Navy concept, units are part of the gaining command. Make them a detachment or department and let the gaining commands provide required administrative support. This action reduces SELRES command structure overhead and allows units to focus By Robert D. Helsel on operations and production.

Officers-in-Charge (OIC) in Place of Commanding Officers (COs):
Make current unit Cos OICs of detachments or department heads and
have them report directly to the gaining command CO. This action
reduces the size and hence the cost of Reserve management staffs required
by Commander, Naval Reserve Surface Forces and Commander, Naval
Reserve Air Forces and their respective regional and area commanders.

Budget: Give the gaining commands budget responsibility and
authority for their SELRES instead of Chief, Naval Reserve Force. This
action would reduce Reserve overhead for budget preparation by the
Director, Naval Reserve.

Stay in Place: Keep officer and enlisted SELRES personnel with one
unit for at least six years (and preferably ten years) before rotation. The
longer they stay, the more they know. The more they know, the more
they can teach to both new reservists and the more frequently rotating
active-duty personnel. Corporate memory has value, and fewer rotations
equal less paperwork.

Personnel

The SELRES officer corps has the experts who can train and manage
others in specific operational and technical functions, whether it be flying an aircraft, programming a computer, or staffing a Joint Chiefs of
Staff paper. If the SELRES program is to maximize its current contribution, then it should consider restructuring its officer corps to be more
like the active-duty limited duty officer program: leaders and doers. This
limited-duty or single-function approach would provide the Navy with
a cadre of operational and technical experts at both officer and enlisted
levels, who have value at mobilization and just as much value now for
routine augmentation.

For this approach to be effective, the Navy must allow its SELRES
officers to use their talents and grade them accordingly. For example, if a
SELRES officer is a professional commercial pilot, do not make him take
a desk job just because he needs his "ticket punched" for promotion; let

him fly and train others to do so. Education, training, and continuity are keys to personnel readiness. A leaner Naval Reserve must capitalize on the leadership and management skills gained by its people outside the military:

If this modification goes into effect, the Navy could take several actions to improve the effectiveness and cost efficiency of SELRES personnel.

Reduce the Number of SELRES Senior Officer Billets (05/06): Drop the running mate concept for SELRES officer promotion. There is nothing wrong with ten-year lieutenants and ten-year lieutenant commanders; after all, ten years of 48 drills per year is only a little more than one full-time man-year. How many lieutenants are ready for promotion after only one year? In the event partial, full, or total mobilization should occur use lineal numbers to match SELRES officers to their active-duty counterpart's grade. Use the savings to keep additional junior officer billets.

Evaluate on Performance: Let the gaining command CO evaluate his SELRES department head/OIC and his officers based on the department/ detachment's mobilization readiness and its direct contribution to the command's operational mission. This action places the emphasis on operational performance and underscores the functional skills of the SELRES officers.

Rotate Officer Positions Within the Unit: Scrap the idea that frequent change broadens the SELRES officer. Unit change can enhance management knowledge but it also can dilute technical skills. Let the senior unit officers exchange duty assignments over the course of their tour. This action provides leadership responsibility and still keeps each officer technically proficient.

Reward SELRES Enlisted Performance (E4-E6): It is just as hard to train and retain qualified technicians and technical supervisors in the SELRES as it is on active duty. Use part of the pay savings from the reduction in senior officer billets to provide cash awards for outstanding performance.

Application

Emphasize Performance: Proposed organizational and personnel changes will reduce SELRES administrative time. Use the additional drill time to master the technical functions and perform the operational mission. Units that drill in their gaining command spaces will be able to perform meaningful tasks more easily than units that drill at other locations. But off-site units are and should be tasked to accomplish meaningful tasks for the gaining command. No more "Victory at Sea" movies.

Mobilization Billets for Active-Duty Personnel: Assign active-duty personnel in shore staff positions mobilization billets with the fleet and use the SELRES to relieve them in crisis situations. When the Navy needs crisis manning, it needs it at sea. The active-duty officer or enlisted who recently left a ship or squadron for his shore tour is more attuned and probably better prepared to re-man than most SELRES. Remember, they also serve who only push paper.

Relieve Active-Duty Personnel Regularly: Schedule and use regular active training periods to learn and perform. Let the active-duty personnel take leave, attend school, or go on an operation. Special augmentation is successful only if routinely practiced.

Mr. Helsel is a commander in the Selected Reserve.

15 "The NRF Has More to Offer"

Lieutenant Commander
William D. Schubert Jr., USNR

U.S. Naval Institute *Proceedings*
(October 1990): 76–77

SQUADRONS ARE MADE UP of both active-duty and Naval Reserve Force (NRF) ships. This causes an inordinate strain on all concerned; as the NRF expands and missions are more clearly defined, a dedicated squadron advocate will become a necessity. Even as things stand today, many of the specialized problems could be handled by an echelon-four staff manned with training and administration of the Naval Reserve (TAR) personnel.

A simple example can be found in the scheduling of NRF ships. With a unified squadron scheduler, drill weekends could be turned into multiship two-day exercises, interacting with Naval Reserve helicopters, P-3s, and submarine/surface targets of opportunity. Although this occurs to a certain extent now (driven in the Northeast by Surface Group Four, for instance), the NRF ship schedules are not written toward this goal, nor is there any systematic use of available weekend assets. A reserve ship squadron participating in quarterly scheduling conferences on an equal footing with its active-duty counterpart could plan for area selected reserve (SelRes) training, rather than fitting the reservists into existing ship schedules.

A unified response to several of the NRF's problems could be coordinated at the echelon-four level and, in some cases, solved. Specifically:

- Personnel Assignment Coordination: A single advocate with a multi-ship perspective could offer assistance. Without the distractions of active-duty deployment cycles, a squadron could close the communication gap for several ships at once. The drawdown cycle is a new challenge for each ship that must face it without prior experience; this is compounded by a lack of real assistance from the regular Navy squadron.

- Officer/Enlisted TAR Training: Some sort of course with minimum competency requirements (Commander Naval Education and Training standards) should be developed to make the TAR community a more consistently knowledgeable specialty. This is in progress at the Naval Reserve Readiness Command/Reserve Center level with the Training Evaluation Board, but it is not extended to shipboard TARs. Echelon-four evaluation and analysis of minimum requirements to effectively administer the SelRes program on NRF ships could develop into a minimum requirement to become a TAR and/or to advance within the designator. This would greatly enhance the active reserve relationship.

- SelRes Logistics/Administrative Support: The resolution of difficulties inherent in tracking, training, and paying someone who is on liberty 28 days per month falls directly on the NRF and, in the case of tracking and paying, flows rapidly downhill to the personnelman first class and yeoman first class, who have active-duty sailors and executive officers clamoring for attention during those 28 days. Different solutions have been tried at the Readiness Commands that own Reserve Centers providing SelRes to NRF ships, but none would approach the effectiveness of a dedicated NRF squadron. Someone has to be accountable for a SelRes at all times (just like active duty), and ships, especially those in the NRF, tend to get under way on short notice or have to respond to events beyond their control (such as a surprise operational propulsion plant examination). When this occurs, both the Reserve Center and the Naval Reserve Readiness Command are frequently too far removed to provide any meaningful assistance, and the SelRes falls in the gap. An NRF squadron would be in a perfect position to predict, insofar as possible, perturbations in an individual ship's schedule. Such a squadron could smooth the transition to an alternate plan.

The most difficult problem is Operations control. Whose orders do I execute? From whom do I take direction? To whom do I report? This is the core of military life: a clear, disciplined organization that prepares for the Chaos of battle or violence of the elements. Neither the ship, dictated to by both Navy and Naval Reserve Force upper echelons, nor the SelRes, whose travel and pay arrangements come from the reserve side and from the ship commanding officer, is clear just who ultimately controls their careers. This is as Political a hot potato as there has ever been. Someone at the very top has to decide what the Potential is for the NRF. Which is the best organization to accomplish the mission? Stretching the reservist and the ship between two camps is unfair and an extraordinary waste of assets in these times when newspaper headlines scream cutbacks.

Few realize the untapped potential of NRF ships. I was assigned to a ship toward the end of her first year of conversion to NRF status, when the personnel crunch was just being felt. There was a good deal of animosity toward the weekend warriors; this continued for the first eight or nine months of my tour. Then something changed. The ship seemed to adjust to the new reality. The crew hadn't really turned over, but SelRes/active-duty interactions seemed to be more productive. I was walking along the pier looking at the ship one Saturday afternoon on a drill weekend when I saw five boatswain's mates working on the dipped anchor. They were in appropriate safety gear, correctly painting haze gray on the properly prepared anchor. They were obviously enjoying the work and doing it well. Not one was active duty. A second-class SelRes was supervising and doing it well. It occurred to me that the ship had made a successful progression that day—it was the first time an unsupervised SelRes team was given a major project. The active-duty deck force, having just returned from a long exercise with many tiring underway replenishments and a lot of long watches, was being relieved of an odious, oft repeated task.

Naval Reserve personnel should be supported with clear, concise directions and goals, with training and administrative assistance, with upper-level communication and policies. We should unite—SelRes and active duty—to become a central part of the next century's Navy.

Lieutenant Commander Schubert is director of administration at Naval Reserve Readiness Command Eight.

16 "Navy's Reserve Will Be Integrated with Active Forces"

Rear Admiral David O. Anderson, USN, and
Rear Admiral J. A. Winnefeld, USN

U.S. Naval Institute *Proceedings*
(November 2004): 61–62

IN THE POST–COLD WAR WORLD, most naval professionals take for granted that investments in platforms, systems, people, and training must be oriented to address asymmetric threats, rapid changes in technology, globalization, and new business realities. These 21st-century warriors live in a world of fast, adaptable, networked forces that must maintain high states of readiness and employ precision weapons with integrated joint and coalition partners. Shifting national demographics, the demands of a more technically oriented force, the high operating tempos of the global war on terrorism, and a tight fiscal environment create new challenges for the way our Navy is manned. Thus, it should surprise no one that Chief of Naval Operations Vern Clark directed our Navy to take a fresh look at the role of the Navy's Reserve and how it integrates with the active forces to operate in this new environment.

The Navy's reserve component (RC) was structured for the Cold War and designed around large-scale mobilizations and relatively slow response times enabled by adequate warning timelines. Over the years, the RC experienced "mission creep" by accepting roles not originally envisioned for reserve forces. Meanwhile, the active component (AC) managed its RC largely by benign neglect, because the reserve operating model simply did not fit with how the Navy operated. The global war on terrorism, with its greater emphasis on use of reserve forces in specialty roles and to sustain the overall effort, demands that the Navy have the right reserve capabilities. It became imperative to restructure and reintegrate the Navy's Reserve into the Navy—to create a properly aligned and integrated total force designed to provide the capabilities outlined in "Sea Power 21" and to support the Fleet Response Plan.

The key step in achieving active-reserve integration is to determine what the AC really needs its RC to do and when the RC needs to do it. Accordingly, last year Admiral Clark tasked Fleet Forces Command to conduct a review of all reserve capabilities required by the AC. This zero-based review laid the groundwork for a more integrated total force in which RC functions directly support "Sea Power 21" missions. Admiral Clark was briefed on the process and product of the review in August 2004.

The zero-based review systematically studied gaps in AC capabilities that should be filled by the RC. Cost and risk values were assigned to each validated reserve capability relative to the active-duty mission so senior leaders could make informed decisions on the appropriate levels of investment. The result was a blend of existing and new capabilities, and some were recommended for realignment or divestment. The review acknowledged two essential types of support the AC will receive from the RC: (1) the Navy has needs that are best filled by discrete units that stand up when required to provide a specific capability, and (2) there is a clear need for individuals or portions of units that can augment existing active commands. Nearly every validated capability is designed to increase the warfighting capacity of the active force. The new validation concept is simply what the AC needs to have, not just what is nice to have.

Activities and commands are now coordinating with claimants and resource sponsors to develop a multiyear transition plan to align their manning requirements to these approved RC functions. In addition, Fleet

Forces Command will be conducting an analysis of existing and future joint requirements. As the culture change required by active-reserve integration begins to take hold in the AC, new opportunities for integration that truly increase the capacity of the active force will emerge that must be addressed.

The Way Ahead

The next step is to give the active-duty forces the ability to access their reserve forces when they need them, to train them the way they want them to be trained, and to report their readiness.

This means the AC will take ownership of the readiness of the RC, with individual active-duty commanding officers clearly understanding they are responsible for the readiness of their supporting reserve forces. The AC will define what training levels the RC will meet, apply metrics to the required RC readiness levels, and oversee RC training.

Good communication is vital to active-reserve integration. The RC has been very successful over the past year in informing its members about the new obligations this integration brings and the Chief of Naval Operations' vision for a total force. It will take strong, involved leadership to ensure our active-duty commanders and commanding officers understand and embrace the notion that their supporting reservists are a daily responsibility and force multiplier. Cultural acceptance on the part of the AC will lead to even stronger acceptance on the part of the RC. A fully integrated active and reserve force will exist only when the AC and RC break through many of their paradigms of the past and realize the art of the possible.

We also must adjust the supporting bureaucracy and structure to eliminate impediments that restrict AC access to its RC. The Navy needs to be able to tap the military and civilian skills that reside within the reserve forces, and the RC must demonstrate flexibility to meet the capabilities required by the fleet. This will mean finding new ways to structure and fund how the reserves are tied to the active force. It is clear that the days of drilling 2 days per month and 14 days per year at a reserve center or conducting convenient exercises are over. We are now a surge Navy, which means that when we need the reserve forces, they must be ready. The message for the reservists is that they need to be prepared to mobilize one or more times during a career—or consider finding a different part-time job. Again, effective communication is critical. As long as families and employers of reservists know their serving family members and employees are making a difference in our nation's security, they will be much more supportive about the reservists deploying. A deployment may be for 30 to 60 days of operational support or it may be for 6 months to 12 months of mobilization.

To support this new construct, RC units requiring tactical skills eventually will be located in the fleet concentration areas. Reserve capabilities in the nation's heartland will focus on skills that are not perishable or that do not require frequent training with the AC to achieve tactical proficiency. The RC structure in the heartland will fill more of the Navy's joint requirements to support the Northern Command and the Strategic Command.

There will be cultural obstacles to active-reserve integration, particularly in areas where the most dramatic changes will occur. It may be years before reserve force integration will be routine. However, the long-overdue focus of this integration will transform the Navy's Reserve into what it was intended all along to be: a valuable force multiplier for our Navy.

Admiral Anderson is Director for Force Integration and **Admiral Winnefeld** is Director for Warfare Programs and Requirements, Fleet Forces Command.

INDEX

Abert, James G., 135
Adams, John, 12
Afghanistan, 6–7
Ahern, John W., 91
aircraft carriers, 113–14
Ames, Alan W., 19
Amphitrite, 15
Anderson, David O., 167
Andrews, Adolphus, 79
antisubmarine ships, WWII: in action, 79–91; effectiveness of, 72–74; life on board, 71–72; ship design and building, 67–71; Subchaser Training Center (SCTC), 74–79
Attack Squadron 702, 108–23
Aviation Ground School at MIT, 24

Bailey, Thomas E., 91
Balkans, 6
Bara, 60
Belich, Adam, 91
Berkey, Jonas M., 80–81
Berlin Crisis (1961), 5
Blackburn, Paul, 107

Bonham, Marion C., 87–88
Bosnia, 9
Boston, 16
Boxer, 112, 115
Braun, Robin, 10
Brown, Wellesley L., 19
Bucklin, Curtis L., 91
Bureau of Naval Personnel, 9
Bush, George W., 6, 8

Callo, Joseph F., 24
Camp Lemonnier (Djibouti), 8
Carrier Air Wing 8, 7
Carusone, Gaetano, 91
Central Command, 6
Chance Vought F41.1 Corsairs, 119
Chapman, Chester J., 91
Cheyenne, 16
Chicago, 15
Churchill, Winston, 62
Cities Service Fuel, 90
Civil War, 13–14
Clark, Vern, 8, 164, 165
Clift, A. Denis, 66

Coast Guard, 99
Combined Joint Task Force–Horn of
   Africa, 8
Concord, 16
Cotton, John, 9

David, Charles R., 91
Davison, F. Trubee, 17–19, 20, 21, 22,
   23, 24
Davison, Henry P., Jr., 19
D-Day, 60–65
Desert Shield, Operation, 6
Desert Storm, Operation, 6
Dione, 67
Director of the Naval Reserve, 101
Ditman, Albert J., 19
"Donald Duck Navy," 78–79, 85
Douglas AD Skyraiders, 119–20
Dow, Albert H., 91
Dubuque, 15
Dunn, Robert F., 146

EA-18G aircraft, 7
Eastern Sea Frontier, 60
Edward L. Doheny, 89
Eisenhower, Dwight D., 61–62, 65
Electric Boat Company, 68
Electronic Attack Squadron 209, 7
11 Princeonians, 24
Elizabeth City Shipyard, 70
Enduring Freedom, Operation, 6–8
Expeditionary Medical Facility
   (Kuwait), 8

Farwell, John V., III, 19
5th Fleet, 6
First Yale Unit, 17–24
The First Yale Unit (Paine), 22
The First Yale Unit (Sims), 17
Fleet Logistics Support Wing squad-
   rons, 7

Fleet Reserve, 104
Forrestal, James V., 24
Fort Dix, 9
Fort Hamilton, 38, 39
Fort Jackson, 9

Gates, Artemus L., 19
Georgia School of Technology, 26
Gilliam, John A., 91
Gloucester, 15
Gould, C.B., 19
Great Lakes, IL, 38
Grumman F9F Panthers, 119
Guy, George H., 91

Haiti, 6
Hampton Roads Naval Air Station, 39
Haner, Harold V., 91
Harvard University, 26
Hayward, Thomas B., 143
Helicopter Combat Support Special
   Squadron 4, 7
Helicopter Combat Support Special
   Squadron 5, 7
Helsel, Robert D., 159

Ice King, 59
individual augmentees (IAs), 8, 9
Ingalls, David S., 16, 19
Inland Reserve Divisions: civic functions of, 54–55; extracurricular
   activities, 51–52; facilities, 55–57;
   officer personnel, 48–49; recruitment, 49–52; reservists' families,
   53–54
Iraqi Freedom, Operation, 7–8
Irwin, Herbert M., 91

James, Daniel V., 81
Jones, Frederick, 21
Jordy, Jules J., 80

King, Ernest J., 60
Knox-class frigates, 143
Korean War, 5, 108–23
Kosovo, 9

Land, Emory S., 59, 60
Lehman, John, 5, 143
Lewandowski, Joseph T., 91
Liney, Charles F., 91
Lovett, Robert A., 19
Luders Marine Construction Company, 68

Marblehead, 15
Marine Corps, 25, 99–100
Marshall, George C., 65
"Mary Ann," 19–20
Massachusetts naval militia, 4, 14–15
Mattis, James, 6
McCommons, Robert W., 91
McCulloch, Dave, 19–20
McCurry, Bennie F., 91
McDaniel, Eugene F., 75–79
McDonnell, Edward, 23
Medal of Honor, 5
medical professionals, 8
Merchant Marine Naval Reserve, 97, 106
merchant mariners, 13, 14
Mexican War, 13
Militia Act of 1792, 12–13
Miller, Harlan B., 155
minesweeping, 138
Moran, Edmond J., 58–66
Morgan, J.P., 15
Mulberry harbors, 62–65

napalm, 114
National Defense Act of 1916, 25
National Defense Authorization Act (2013), 10

NATO Role III Medical Unit (Kandahar), 8
Naval Academy, U.S., 42, 48–49
Naval Air Facility Washington, D.C., 7
Naval Air Station Dallas, 108–10
Naval Air Station North Island, 110–12
Naval Air Station Whidbey Island, 7
Naval Appropriations Act of 1920, 96
Naval Auxiliary Reserve, 95
Naval Coast Defense Reserve, 95
Naval Control of Shipping, 138
naval medical reserve corps, 16
Naval Reserve Act of 1938, 98–99
Naval Reserve Aviation: aviation cadet program, 41; Aviation Ground School at MIT, 24; bases, 43–44; 11 Princeonians, 24; establishment of, 37–39; fatal accident rate, 41–42; First Yale Unit, 17–24; in Korean War, 108–23; Naval Reserve Flying Corps, 19, 22, 37; squadrons, 44; status pre-WWII, 40–45
Naval Reserve Flying Corps, 19, 22, 37, 95
Naval Reserve Force, 4, 16
Naval Reserve Force ships scheduling, 160–63
Naval Reserve Inspection Board, 101
Naval Reserve Officers' Training Corps (ROTC), 106; costs, 32–34; coursework, 27–32; employment prospects, 34–35; establishment, 25–26; graduate compensation, 30–31; objectives of, 26
Naval War College, 129
Navy Expeditionary Medical Unit at Landstuhl RMC, 8
Navy Reserve: active duty for work, 128–29; active-reserve integration, 8–9, 137–38, 145, 162–63, 164–67;

demobilization after WWI, 93–97; demobilization planning after WWII, 99–107; divisions of, 102–6; excessive seniority, 148–49; Fleet Reserve, 104; future concerns and emphases, 9–11; inception, 3–4, 16, 95; Individual Ready Reserve (IRR) status, 154; Inland Reserve Divisions, 47–57, 155; in Korean War, 5; logistics and administrative support, 161–62; Merchant Marine Reserve, 106; officer promotion system, 151–55, 158; in Operation Enduring Freedom, 6–8; in Operation Iraqi Freedom, 7–8; Operations control, 162; organization of, 101–2, 156–57, 162; Organized Reserve, 102–4; patriotism of reservists, 138–39; peacetime contributory work, 125–34; peacetime peak load uses, 129–32; personnel turnover, 148; personnel usage, 157–58; Readiness unit program, 153; recruiting, 144–45; reforms to, 151–55, 156–59, 160–63; renaming of, 9; reserve missions, 127–28; specialized civilian skills of, 132–34, 157–58; training and administration (TAR) of, 139–44, 160, 161; in Vietnam War, 5; Volunteer Reserve, 104–6; Volunteer Training Units, 148; in World War II, 4–5
Navy Reserve Force, 9
New York Aerial Police, 38
9/11, 6
Northwestern University, 26

O'Donnell, Edward, 86, 87
Oliver Hazard Perry-class frigates, 143
Olivieri, Paul, 91
OPNAV, 9

Organized Reserve, 102–4
O'Rourke General Classification Test, 50
Ozark, 15

P-8A Poseiden aircraft, 10
PC 1123, 87
Pearson, George A., 91
Pennsylvania, 30
Pensacola, FL, 39–40, 41
Perkins, George A., 91
Plymouth, 90
Privateers and Volunteers (Stivers), 12

Ramsey, Bertram, 63
Ready Mariner program, 144
Reagan, Ronald, 5
Revolutionary War, 12
Reynolds, Thomas, 58
Rieffel, Louis B., 91
Rivers, Henry, 87
Rodgers, 15
Roosevelt, Franklin D., 67
ROTC. *See* Naval Reserve Officers' Training Corps (ROTC)
R.P. Resor, 84
Rudy, Ellis E., 91

SC 437, 85
SC 507, 83–84
SC 540, 85
SC 638, 80
SC 656, 85–87
SC 682, 88–90
SC 704, 70
SC 983, 84–85
SC 989, 87
SC 998, 85
SC 1024, 89–91
SC 1039, 80–81
SC 1279, 82–83
SC 1330, 87–88

SC 1354, 82
SC 1470, 87
SC-438 class subchaser, 68, 71
SC-449 class subchaser, 68
SC-450 class subchaser, 68
SC-453 class subchaser, 68
SC-497 class subchasers, 68–70
Schubert, William D., Jr., 163
Sea and Air Mariner (SAM) program, 144–45
"Sea Power 21," 165
Sea Scouts, 29
Second Yale Unit, 24
Sims, William S., 17
Somers, 15
Soviet Union, 5
Spanish-American War, 4, 15
Spicer, Ray C., 91
Squantum, MA, 38, 39
Stalin, Josef, 62
Stark, Harold R., 60
state naval militias, 4, 15–16, 49
Stivers, Reuben E., 12
Stopp, William H., 91
Strike Fighter Squadron 201, 7
Sturtevant, Albert D., 17, 19
subchasers. *See* antisubmarine ships, WWII
Sullivan, Ed, 83–84
Swasey, Alfred Loring, 67

Task Force 17, 112
Task Force 58 (Marines), 6
Task Force 77, 112, 119
Taylor, Joseph E., 91
Taylor, Lieutenant, 84
Tennessee, 30

terrorism, global war on, 165
Theodore Roosevelt (CVN-71), 7
Thompson, 65
Toledo, 118–19
Towers, John, 22
training and administration of reservists (TAR), 139–41

U-578, 84
U-boats. *See* antisubmarine ships
University of California, 26, 30, 34–35
U.S. Fleet Forces Command, 9, 10
USCG 83421, 88

Vanderbilt, Harold, 60
Vernor, W.H., 123–24
Vietnam War, 5
Volunteer Aerial Coast Patrol No. 1, 21
Volunteer Aerial Coast Patrol No. 2, 24
Volunteer Naval Reserve, 95
Volunteer Reserve, 97
Volunteer Training Units, 148
Vorys, John M., 19

Wanamaker, Rodman, 20
War of 1812, 12
Ward (DD-139), 4
Watkins, James D., 143
Wellfleet, 89
Williams, Warren, Jr., 91
Wiman, Charles D., 19
Winnefeld, J.A., 167
Winter, John, 88
World War I, 4, 16, 17–24, 37
World War II, 4–5, 79–91

Yale University, 26

SERIES EDITOR

THOMAS J. CUTLER has been serving the U.S. Navy in various capacities for more than fifty years. The author of many articles and books, including several editions of *The Bluejacket's Manual* and *A Sailor's History of the U.S. Navy,* he is currently the director of professional publishing at the Naval Institute Press and Fleet Professor of Strategy and Policy with the Naval War College. He has received the William P. Clements Award for Excellence in Education as military teacher of the year at the U.S. Naval Academy, the Alfred Thayer Mahan Award for Naval Literature, the U.S. Maritime Literature Award, and the Naval Institute Press Author of the Year Award.

The Naval Institute Press is the book-publishing arm of the U.S. Naval Institute, a private, nonprofit, membership society for sea service professionals and others who share an interest in naval and maritime affairs. Established in 1873 at the U.S. Naval Academy in Annapolis, Maryland, where its offices remain today, the Naval Institute has members worldwide.

Members of the Naval Institute support the education programs of the society and receive the influential monthly magazine *Proceedings* or the colorful bimonthly magazine *Naval History* and discounts on fine nautical prints and on ship and aircraft photos. They also have access to the transcripts of the Institute's Oral History Program and get discounted admission to any of the Institute-sponsored seminars offered around the country.

The Naval Institute's book-publishing program, begun in 1898 with basic guides to naval practices, has broadened its scope to include books of more general interest. Now the Naval Institute Press publishes about seventy titles each year, ranging from how-to books on boating and navigation to battle histories, biographies, ship and aircraft guides, and novels. Institute members receive significant discounts on the Press' more than eight hundred books in print.

Full-time students are eligible for special half-price membership rates. Life memberships are also available.

For a free catalog describing Naval Institute Press books currently available, and for further information about joining the U.S. Naval Institute, please write to:

Member Services
U.S. NAVAL INSTITUTE
291 Wood Road
Annapolis, MD 21402-5034
Telephone: (800) 233-8764
Fax: (410) 571-1703
Web address: www.usni.org